Strange Minnesota Monsters

STRANGE MINNESOTA MONSTERS

CHRISTOPHER LARSEN

Schiffer Publishing Ltd

4880 Lower Valley Road • Atglen, Pennsylvania 19310

Schiffer Books are available at special discounts for bulk purchases for sales promotions or premiums. Special editions, including personalized covers, corporate imprints, and excerpts can be created in large quantities for special needs. For more information contact the publisher:

Published by Schiffer Publishing Ltd.
4880 Lower Valley Road
Atglen, PA 19310
Phone: (610) 593-1777; Fax: (610) 593-2002
E-mail: Info@schifferbooks.com

For the largest selection of fine reference books on this and related subjects, please visit our web site at **www.schifferbooks.com**
We are always looking for people to write books on new and related subjects. If you have an idea for a book please contact us at the above address.

This book may be purchased from the publisher.
Include $5.00 for shipping.
Please try your bookstore first.
You may write for a free catalog.

In Europe, Schiffer books are distributed by
Bushwood Books
6 Marksbury Ave.
Kew Gardens
Surrey TW9 4JF England
Phone: 44 (0) 20 8392-8585; Fax: 44 (0) 20 8392-9876
E-mail: info@bushwoodbooks.co.uk
Website: www.bushwoodbooks.co.uk

All text by by Christopher Larsen

Photos by Christopher Larsen unless otherwise noted

permissions for www.monstropedia.com: "There is no agreement or understanding between you and Monstropedia regarding your use or modification of this information beyond the GNU Free Documentation License (GFDL)..."

Library of Congress Control Number: 2010929454

Designed by RoS
Type set in Perdition/Korinna BT
ISBN: 978-0-7643-3598-3
Printed in The United States of America

DEDICATION

To those who explore the unknown, expanding
the known, and to the monsters who make things
interesting when you least expect it.

Acknowledgments

I'd like to acknowledge those who have contributed to the writing of this book, specifically to all of the individuals through emails, Internet, phone, and personal visits that I interviewed. Thanks for taking the time to tell me your stories, no matter how difficult and frightening it was. I'd also like to thank Bill, and my brother, Erik, for supporting my crazy ideas about monster hunting.

I'd also like to thank my editor, Dinah Roseberry at Schiffer Publishing, for giving me the chance to write such a fun and exciting book! Lastly, kudos go to my wife, Nancy, and my two boys, Zach and Alex. I write from the heart, which is where they are always.

CONTENTS

FOREWORD

NIETZSCHE ONCE SAID, "I have seen the face of the monster, and he is us…" or maybe it was Damien H., the creepy kid who lived down the road from us. Regardless, my brother and I grew up on an extremely isolated farm outside of (ironically) Farmington, Minnesota. With five decaying outbuildings, along with acres of uninhabited farmland surrounding us and immense imaginations, we spent a lot of time and effort talking about, imagining, and eventually writing about monsters. Armed with ropes, hooks, and tennis shoes that could miraculously stick spider-like to the slick aluminum roofs, we climbed up to survey this magical land, wondering in our hearts whether even Tolkien himself could have dreamed up a more dangerously exciting landscape.

So when my brother, Chris, called me up and said: "Hey, let's drive three hours, tromp through the late November woods of the Superior National Forest, freeze our butts off, and search for Bigfoot," I said *no*. Then he said he'd buy the beer, so I said *yes*.

So we set off. Fueled by

A drawing of a reptilian lizard man, reported to inhabit southeastern Minnesota and southwestern Wisconsin.

alcohol-induced warmth and a headlamp that he had mysteriously "forgot to change the battery" in, we headed into the woods of Northern Minnesota to try to capture some evidence of the elusive Bigfoot. We set up a trail camera, used the night vision goggles and thermal scanner. It was an impromptu trip, so, as was probably expected, we didn't find much. But for a brief few hours, as we walked the state trail, we talked about the best way to find the creature, debating different types of equipment, bandying about theories and conjectures as to where and when would be the best time to track it. I say all this only to point out that never once did we question whether or not the beast of legend actually existed... that was beyond fact.

After a whirlwind exploration that included a few hours of ghost hunting at a cemetery strangely located next to the AmericInn we were staying at, we settled back into the hotel, tired, sore, hungry, and even a little bit disappointed. After a fitful sleep, we once again mounted the trail, making sure that no monster footprints had eluded us in the deep, darkening night, or that there weren't tufts of fur ripped off by jagged trees. In the end, though, Bigfoot was not to be found.

You may think that you need some sort of special skill or University degree to investigate monsters, but it is exactly the contrary. Sure it helps to have helicopters, thermal imaging equipment, expensive cameras, or even a headlamp that works... but the simple truth is this: If you have an interest in knowing the unknown and feeling the adrenalin surge as you investigate the dark corners of the land, then that makes you a monster hunter... no equipment or special degree necessary.

Some may think it silly to go chasing after monsters. But in a world where so much evil is perpetrated by monsters of the human kind, isn't it nice to sit back and imagine a world where the worst thing might be a overly hairy, bipedal herbivore that occasionally turns up at the edges of the untouched natural forest?

~E. John Larsen
Brother, author, and one who ponders the last immortal words
of Socrates: "I drank what?"
November, 2009

Do You Believe in Monsters?

"There are very few monsters who warrant the fear we have of them."

– Andre Gide (French writer, humanist and moralist, 1947 Nobel Prize for literature)

Do you believe in monsters? Now there's a loaded question. Like most excellent questions, the answer tends to be, "it depends." In this case, it depends on what type of monster you're talking about. If it's the kind that goes on a shooting spree at your local mall during a busy lunchtime, or the kind that run airplanes into the World Trade Centers, then the answer would be a resounding *yes*. But, if we are talking more about the things that go bump in the night, the lurkers and shadowy slithering things that never quite seem to be associated with most people's reality, well, then the answer might be a bit more difficult.

Unless of course you've seen a monster.

But for most of you, perhaps we can spend a moment discussing and dissecting the possibility that hairy hulking monsters exist. And to do that, I believe we must determine the category of monsters associated with darkness and mayhem, quantifying them and allowing you to perhaps better tackle the question, "do you believe in monsters?"

For instance, there's a big difference between Bigfoot and a Big Cat. Or how about elves? All of these which are contained within this book (and in Minnesota, of course), might be considered to have different levels of strangeness. Which hits on a key point in this book; the monsters we will talk about focus more on being strange, rather than malicious and bent on causing destruction. Except for the ones that might eat you, of course.

That does not mean the monsters contained within this book are cute and cuddly; they are far from that. No, some of the creatures explained within these pages come from the deepest and darkest side of reality. But let's look further into the categories of monsters. Perhaps we'll get a better idea of what they are, and whether you believe in them.

As previously indicated, there are monsters among humans, and humans that are monsters. For the most part (with the exception of the Wendigo Psychosis), we will not discuss the situation in which a human becomes a monster, at least to the extent where there isn't any physical transformation occurring. Mass murders, serial killers, and suicidal terrorists are monsters, in my opinion, but do not transform their physical appearance. What we will discuss, is the nonhuman monsters—the strange ones at that.

The other thing to remember is that monsters are not a new phenomena; they have been around since the beginning, since humans have dreamt and feared the unknown. Which to me, hits on an important subject—the relationship between monsters and the emotional aspects of fear, specifically the fear of the unknown. That, in fact, could be the basic definition of what a monster is, that you can define a monster as something you don't know about, or can't understand, or perhaps don't want to understand.

In Wikipedia (the ultimate source of information, truthful or not), it says the word "monster" derives from Latin meaning "omen," from the root of "to warn." But it also can mean "prodigy," or "miracle."

I checked an online dictionary for the definition of monsters. It describes monsters in several different ways:

1. A legendary animal combining features of animal and human form or having the forms of various animals in combination.

2. Any creature so ugly or monstrous as to frighten people.

3. Any animal or human grotesquely deviating from the normal shape, behavior, or character.

4. A person who excites horror by wickedness, cruelty, etc.

5. Any animal or thing huge in size.

6. An animal or plant of abnormal form or structure, as from marked malformation or the absence of certain parts or organs.

7. Anything unnatural or monstrous.

So you see, there are many ways we can look at things and determine if something is a monster or not. But to me, the central theme in all of this is to have a creature that is completely different from the norm; one that is unusual or unknown.

CATEGORY OF MONSTERS

One of my favorite websites to search for information on monsters is www.monstropedia.com. They have just about any strange monster you can think of. And they've categorized them into the following buckets of terror:

ANGELS AND DEMONS

Angels, Ars Goetia, Bogeyman, and Fallen Angels.

ARTIFICIAL MONSTERS

Frankenstein monsters, Genetically-engineered monsters, Magical monsters, and Mechanoids.

CORPOREAL UNDEAD

Death deities, Ghouls, Omens, Psychopomps, Undead, Vampires, Zombies.

CRYPTIDS AND DINOSAURS

Creatures studied by Cryptozoology, the science that supports the existence of elusive and rare creatures. Subcategories are Avian monsters, Bipedal monsters, Carnivorous mammals, Dinosaurs, Herbivorous mammals, Hoaxes, Primates and hominids, Reptilian monsters, Sea and Lake monsters.

FAIRY CREATURES

Creatures mostly with a Celtic origin. Subcategories are Dwarves, Elves, Fairy animals, Giants, Goblins, Household spirits, Nature spirits, Nymphs, Subterraneans, and Water spirits.

HUMAN MONSTERS

Humans like Charles Manson, Jack the Ripper, Vlad The Impaler, basically people who do monstrous things. Subcategories are: Cannibals, Diseases, Freaks, Heroes, Homicidal maniacs, Legendary races, Serial killers, Witches and warlocks.

PARANORMAL ENTITIES

Paranormal, supernatural, and extraterrestrial entities. Sub-categories include: Extraterrestrials, Ghosts, Protective spirits, Shadows, Spectral animals, and possibly Subterraneans.

FABULOUS BEASTS

Unbelievable beasts of size and stature. Subcategories are: Animals, Dragons, Ground beasts, Hybrids, Legendary races, Sea and lake monsters, Vegetals, and Winged creatures.

SHAPESHIFTERS

Animen, humans morphing into animals and monstrous totemic animals. Subcategories are: Felines, Hags, Snake people, Werewolves.

The above classification is one example of many on how to categorize monsters. Some of them, such as ghosts, I would not necessarily define as a monster. It would depend on the type of ghost (or type of haunting). Still, all of the above monsters fit the definition of strange or unknown. And you will find, as you read this book, the Minnesota monsters fit nicely into one or more of the categories above.

So is all this stuff about monsters alarming? Should you lock your doors at night, sleep with a necklace of garlic, and a gun with a silver nitrate bullet under your pillow? That's entirely up to you. But you may want to think through the likelihood of a nightmarish creature visiting you anytime soon. First of all, have you ever seen a monster, or any strange creature of the night (other than your Uncle Albert raiding the fridge at 1 a.m.)? Do you know of anyone who has? If the answer is *no* to both, then you will probably never run into one. But not a guarantee, that's for sure.

You will find out, however, through reading this book, that there are many people around the globe who have experienced something supernatural, something monstrous in the night. And the stories, based on true events, are in your own backyard, found throughout the state of Minnesota. So like it or not, the monsters are apparently here, lurking in the shadows. Will they visit you? Who knows. My guess, however, is that if you invite them, they will come.

As for my life experiences with monsters, I have to say there's not many I've met (sorry Uncle Albert, you're not the monstrous Eatamus Fridget-arous). The closest I've come is with the shadow people. Yes, like many, I've seen things from the corner of my eye, a dark, formless mass, darting across a room. But Bigfoot? I've never seen one. Although I feel like a hairy Bigfoot sometimes,

Cerberus, from ancient Greek and Roman mythology, quite possibly a distant ancestor to the current Black Dog and Hellhound sightings.

with all that hair growing in places it shouldn't, accept on the top of my head (in the sun no less). Which makes me wonder, does Bigfoot go bald, not to mention senile? If so, perhaps there is a chance someday to capture the beast, as he wanders clueless down the I-494 median in rush hour, scratching his head and wondering where all the trees, nuts, and berries went.

The only other time I've dealt with monsters, is when I was a child, trying to go to bed at night. And as many children still believe, there was a bogeyman in my closet. I could sense him in there, even when the door was closed (and it was always closed by the way, unless my mom left it open—how could she do such a thing!). But there never was any monster in my room, right? Just the wild imagination of a little boy. Well, can you prove there wasn't?

As I eluded to earlier, the fear of monsters, as it were, stems from one's fear of the unknown. In that case, the bogeyman was a symbol of that which was not known to me, right? But was it real? If you would have asked me when I was ten, I would have said absolutely, along with Santa Claus, the Easter Bunny, and the Tooth Fairy.

Reality, as it seems, is in the mind of the beholder. I believed in such things when I was young, therefore at the time they were as real as they needed to be. But now? Well, the fears of the unknown, as an adult, are much different; they are more concrete, dealing more with the physical unknowns, like money, health, and whether or not the Vikings will ever win a Super Bowl. Or if Brett Farve is mixed up in some cheese-head conspiracy to get the Packers in the Super Bowl one more time.

A Very Brief History of Monsters

Perhaps this is a good time to delve into the history of monsters. I won't touch on all the multitude of beasts, but will attempt to give you a basic idea of where some of them came from, and where some of them might be going. If you want an indepth discussion on the history, you'll need to find a different book. This book is more about the stories and real-life events with monsters.

And let's not forget about new monsters being found (or possibly created, in the subconscious psyche of humanity). After all, Freddie Krueger from *Nightmare on Elm Street* wasn't around a hundred years ago, neither was Jason from *Friday the 13th*. Or were they? Perhaps Freddie and Jason were always there, just waiting to be discovered once again and brought into the mainstream of monsters. And I'm sure there will be some new monsters in the near future. They always seem to be reinventing themselves.

Monsters, as I have indicated, have been part of our lives since the beginning. It does not matter what culture, or what part of the world you come from; monsters in one form or another are there. Whether you see them on cave paintings from the Hopewell Native American cultures, or the scrolls of ancient China, or the Hieroglyphics of the Egyptian Pyramids, the monsters and the fear of the unknown is prevalent (it's hard, however, to prove the monsters were physically there). If you're a follower of Joseph Campbell, and his Power of Myth, you would understand then that monsters, when incorporated into a myth, transcends the boundaries of the physical world, interconnecting at a subconscious level. Psychoanalyst Carl Jung also had similar beliefs, where regardless of location in the world, people had certain tendencies to form the same mythic symbols—monsters included.

In ancient times, references to monsters were found in many myths, as mythological creatures. Medusa, Sirens, Cyclopes, and Minotaur are creatures from Greek mythology (which the Romans also assimilated).

These monsters are considered classics, the ones that apparently terrorized our ancestors over two millennium ago. As scary as the monsters we have in our present time, I can't imagine the horrific feeling there would be, having a Cyclops running you down for its next meal.

The Vikings, or Norse mythology, has its own set of monsters, coming from the land of Asgaard and the god Odin, and his home Valhalla. Fenrir the gigantic wolf, Jormungandr the sea-serpent, Huginn and Muninn the ravens. Or how about the evil monster Grendel, in Beowulf. Elves, dwarves, and wizards are also prevalent in Norse mythology, and much more common. Much of J.R.R. Tolkien's Middle Earth stemmed from Norse mythology.

Over in North America, the Native Americans have their own monsters to deal with. The Wendigo (which is one of the stories in this book) is one such fiendish, man-eating creature. There are also skinwalkers, and even Bigfoot may have its origins buried in Native American folklore (among other cultures). And one of my personal favorites, is the Flying Head of the Iroquois. It is a huge hungry head with wings of flapping hair, fiery eyes, and knife-blade teeth. Now that's something you don't want to meet, waking up in your tent from a peaceful night of camping.

There are, of course, numerous other monsters from the past, passed down through history in verbal or written stories. The real question is, which ones are true? Well, that's part of the reason why I wrote this book. I would like to capture information through interviews, other books, the Internet, and my own investigations. Then, perhaps it will help in the future to decipher what was real, and what was not. If anything, this book may at least spark your interest in the supernatural, for you to begin your own investigations and fieldtrips. After all, the best teacher of knowledge is experience itself.

Does that mean all the stories in this book actually happened? It's hard to say. The stories are based on real events. But even the events could have been made up (but not by my doing). With monsters, there is little to no evidence found, other than your occasional Bigfoot print, or grainy picture or video.

It seems, the only way to really know if the monsters exist, is to go out and find them. Which I don't recommend trying, unless you're a professional at it. Of course, the last time I checked, there are no professional monster hunters listed in the phone book. So I guess you're on your own. Just make sure you have plenty of business cards, titled "PROFESSIONAL MONSTER HUNTER." They may help keep the monsters at bay, not to mention the authorities (yeah, right).

The reality is that it will most likely be difficult to accurately prove that any of these monsters exist, unless we have more individuals researching, investigating, and discussing the reports and claims of those who have seen them. And if there is an increase in investigations, we would hopefully have an increase in reports. But we can also do some armchair sleuthing, as I call it. Let's do some theorizing about monsters.

A drawing of a Merman, from Greek mythology, also common in Irish, Finnish, and other mythologies. The real question is if they still exist today, able to live in large bodies of fresh water such as Mille Lacs Lake, Red Lake, or Lake Superior.

So, if we were to assume Bigfoot is real (which in my opinion is not that far of a stretch), we first need to think about how it could survive. As far as I know, any creature living on this earth, needs some basic essentials—food, water, clothing, shelter. For Bigfoot, I'm guessing the clothing part is taken care of, what with the enormous amount of hairs that supposedly cover its body. And as for shelter, there are reports that it will build giant nests of grass and branches to sleep in, or hide out in caves. Water is abundant in the northern regions of Minnesota (and most of Minnesota for that matter). Food is ample as well, being that the creature is apparently an herbivore (although some reports indicate it may in fact be an omnivore like us humans).

It would appear as though Bigfoot could easily exist. The only remaining question, is why we haven't run into one—why haven't we captured more evidence? To me, there are only two obvious answers. One, is that the creature does not in fact exist (which would be way too boring of an answer, as far as I'm concerned). The second answer is that the creature has magical abilities, to disappear and reappear at will, and to mysteriously cover up its tracks, or to become invisible when needed.

There is a third answer, where the Bigfoot population is just too sparse. Perhaps there are only a few of them left in existence. But then, why would that be? Most species, when placed in an environment they can thrive in, multiply like rabbits. I would assume the only predator for Bigfoot would be humans (with big guns, or possibly double Whoppers with cheese), and since nobody has claimed to have captured or killed a Bigfoot (although check the chapter on the Iceman), it would seem there's not too many of them around.

Bigfoot is just one example. What about lake monsters (not to be confused with sea monsters, which are currently extinct in Minnesota)? This seems even less likely, being that most lakes are not large enough to support the eating habits of a large creature. There are a few exceptions, such as Mille Lacs Lake, or most certainly Lake Superior. Yet, there are not too many lake monster stories coming from them. It is interesting, however, that Pepie the Lake Monster, from Lake Pepin (see the lake monster chapter in this book for more information), could possibly travel up and down the Mississippi River, finding lots of food to eat (but the locks and dams would surely slow her down, especially if she doesn't have a passport, or is carrying zebra mussels).

I'm not saying that monsters do not exist; I'm only stating the obvious—it seems very unlikely they do (which depends heavily on your interpretation of what a monster is of course). Yet, tens of thousands of people around the globe have reported over the years strange occurrences of creatures they cannot explain. But their proof is not concrete, and we are left neither proving their existence, or denying it. We're faced with the slim possibility that a monster could be there, right behind you, watching you watch television, or walking down the sidewalk late at night. But don't worry, as long as you don't turn around, you'll be fine.

One crusader for the proof of monsters is the television show *MonsterQuest* on the History channel. Based out of Minnesota, the producers and crew have spent several years traveling across the country gathering data, interviewing people, and investigating on their own, dozens of proposed monster sightings. If you are at all interested in the subject of monsters, I highly recommend watching a few episodes. They may turn you from a skeptic to a believer. What's even more fun, is that they have a video game you can buy, to have fun doing your own monster hunting (in the comforts of your computer and chair). Definitely an enjoyable way to pass the time away at night while you're having trouble sleeping—but that would depend on how scary the virtual monster you're searching for is.

Another show I thoroughly enjoy watching is *Supernatural*, on the SyFy channel. While this does not involve real monster hunting, it certainly is entertaining to watch how Hollywood envisions it. It's great for any monster hunting wannabes, and especially if you like soap operas. I've watched the first couple seasons, and excitedly got into what was happening. It was fun to even imitate the two main characters (who are brothers), by having my brother and I go on a monster hunt together. Sort of like life imitating art I suppose. Regardless, it was a blast hunting monsters (see the field trip section of the Bigfoot chapter).

One other thing to mention, is that I stayed away from putting ghost stories in this book. If you want those, read my other book, *Ghosts of Southeastern Minnesota*. I decided that ghosts fit into their own category, outside of your typical monsters. In particular, ghosts seem to be a dime a dozen, haunting the minds of many. Seems like there are tons of people claiming to see ghosts. But monsters? Not too many of them. And by monsters I mean the physical ones, living and breathing on this earth (and adore fine chocolates, can wear sharp looking hats, and tune a television without the use of ectoplasm).

So there you have it. A basic intro to monsters. Hopefully, I have intrigued you enough to keep reading (or to buy the book if you're standing right now in an isle of the Barnes and Noble bookstore), but not too much to scare you off. In one form or another, I believe certain monsters do exist. The question is, what do we do about it? I'm thinking you have three choices. One is to ignore them and go on with your life (which is what most people do, and what the monsters want you to do, in between their freakish games of demonic Parcheesi). The second is to freak out and declare the world is ending due to mutant frogs inhabiting the earth, along with a platoon of Bigfoots (or would that be Bigfeet?), Wendigos, little mischievous elves, and a few thousand Hoop Snakes.

The third option, which is the most exciting in my opinion, is to find out if they really do exist. Do your own investigation, tracking down the beasts of the night. Which is why I included the next chapter, for those of you who dare venture forth into the night, attempting to discover the ominous inner folds of the forbidden darkness, the unknown worlds hidden from our mundane and monotonous lives. But be careful—you may open up a door to a new reality, one that is not so easily closed.

MONSTER HUNTING 101

"He who fights with monsters might take care lest he thereby become a monster. And if you gaze for long into an abyss, the abyss gazes also into you."

- Friedrich Nietzsche

When I first decided I would put together a chapter on how to monster hunt, I thought it was a good idea. But then I realized it could be the worst thing I ever did. I mean, what if everyone went out in the dead of night, trying to capture a monster? And what might they find? Would it change the world forever? Possibly. But my biggest concern was safety.

There are certain rules you should follow when monster hunting. Safety is numero uno mon capitan. It doesn't matter what kind of monsters you find (even microscopic nanobugs could be deadly), or what kind of evidence; if you aren't safe in your hunting, you could wind up dead. Which means you'll not only lose any proof you might have captured, but also your life. No amount of evidence is worth it, if it costs your life, because then you couldn't stand back and appreciate your findings. Or worse yet, you could become a monster yourself, and who knows who else would then be carrying the monster baton.

Collecting solid evidence is the second thing to remember. Too many times we have someone claim to have seen a monster, talking up an incredible story, but they have nothing to back their claim. A story is great, explaining in detail what you saw. But without a picture, video, or hair samples, well, it's just a story.

The third thing required in monster hunting, like everything in life should be, is to have fun. By fun I don't mean drinking alcoholic beverages and terrorizing the campers sleeping soundly nearby, but to quietly enjoy the nighttime experience—the thrill of tracking down and finding the unknown.

Let's assume you want to do some monster hunting. And by monster hunting, I don't mean you find and kill the beast. It's really more about monster observing. A good picture is worth a thousand words, not to mention way easier to get, than to bring down some mysterious creature and haul it back to civilization. I suppose it's more eco-friendly as well, just like taking pictures of trophy fishes that many do. You can take that Bigfoot picture to your local taxidermist, and ask them to make a replica. I would love to see the look on the taxidermist's face.

A monster born of a ewe, drawn by French explorer Louis Feuillee after seeing it on his trip to South America in the early 1700s.

Tools to Use

There are a variety of tools to use when monster hunting. Most of which depend on what type of monster you are looking for. For instance, bringing a motorboat to look for a Wendigo might not be too useful. And swimming swiftly through the water naked, singing incantations (see Wendigo chapter for more details), will probably not help you capture a lake monster.

Regardless, below are some tools that may be useful on your monster hunt:

Picture Camera

Need I say anything for this one? As I've said, a picture is worth a thousand words. Just make sure you have one of the nicer cameras, with a minimum of 5 megapixels. A good optical zoom is essential—20x or better. That way, when you're several hundred yards away from the creature (a very safe distance I might add), you can zoom in on the beast later and not have that grainy of a resolution. And trail cameras (ones mounted to a tree and have motion sensor and infrared lights) are very useful, to capture the beast while you are away.

Video Camera

The quintessential device used to capture the nefarious monsters in action (whatever it is they do). More recently, digital video cameras have become the norm in most cases, with great resolution available as well. Another key to video cameras, is that it allows you to capture audio of the monster snorting and howling while it does whatever it does in the wild.

Stakes

Stakes are listed *not* as something you use to kill vampires with. I repeat, *no vampire killing*. They're for your tent or canopy, to keep it from flying away in the wind. Wooden stakes to kill the dreaded vampire beast is not recommended. A gun is much more useful, but not recommended either. I would recommend it better to take pictures from a distance. Remember—you're hunting monsters for photos and video, not to go down in history as the guy that plugged Bigfoot full of lead.

Tent

The obvious essential to any outdoor hunting. But most importantly, it is used to lure evil beasts out of hiding. To them, it's like a Christmas package neatly wrapped underneath a tree—with you inside as the perfect present.

And if you're wrapped snugly in a sleeping bag, it's a package within a package for the monster.

BOAT AND SONAR

Definitely needed when hunting lake-type monsters. Not recommended for things like Wendigos, elves, Bigfoot, and any other land-loving creatures. And you don't need a huge boat, but something bigger than the lake monster is most desirable.

BAIT

Unfortunately, in most cases, *you* are the bait. But when using trail cameras, it would be better to have fruit or meat, set out for the monster to eat. Sitting motionless in front of a trail camera for hours is not recommended.

EMF DETECTOR

An Electro Magnetic Field Detector measures electromagnetic radiation. This device is a standard for any ghost hunting being done, but often overlooked for monster hunting. The reason I include it here is just in case the monster you are hunting exhibits paranormal abilities, which would feed off any electronic equipment you have nearby. Of course, if that were the case, there's probably not much hope in you surviving. Hunting supernatural monsters can get real ugly real fast.

DIGITAL AUDIO RECORDER

My personal favorite (and I've named mine – D.A.R.R.E.N. – which stands for Digital Audio Recorder of Really Eerie Noises). A simple device used to capture anomalies in the audio frequency range. Great to have several of these running to be used as secondary measurements. Make sure you "tag" things that happen, i.e. if you cough, state shortly afterward that it was you coughing. Or, if you see a monster and you scream like a little girl, note that as well.

CANDLES AND MATCHES

Obviously used for light – especially after you've lost your flashlight in the forest somewhere, or left it in the car, or back

The classic Griffin, from ancient mythology, with the body of a lion and the head and wings of an eagle.

at home. The matches are good for lighting a fire, to warm you and to keep the monsters away. Just don't try lighting a fire in your tent. Monsters don't like their bait cooked.

COMPASS OR GPS

A compass is great, to help find your way through the forest, but also back to your car. GPS (Global Positioning System) is great as well, because you can then set waypoints, marking the locations you have been (and noting what occurred there).

FLASHLIGHT

Yep. Always needed while hunting monsters. I'd bring one you can wear on your head. That way it's less likely you will drop it while running away from the mysterious and demonic sounds of the night. That's assuming you're hunting at night. Hunting monsters during the day is for sissies.

EXTRA BATTERIES

A no-brainer. Especially needed if paranormal events drain your initial batteries in your flashlight and camera.

GARLIC, HOLY WATER, CRUCIFIX, ETC.

There's a long list of things you could bring on a monster hunt, based on watching movies and television shows such as *Nightstalker*, or *Supernatural*. But for the most part, I believe none of them will work, unless you have the faith to back them up. In which case, you probably don't need the artifact anyway. Garlic could still be useful, however, if you're making pot roast in your Dutch oven, and holy water could always be used if you've run out of your normal water rations.

PEPPER SPRAY

This is excellent to have with you in case you run into a bear (black bear only – grizzlies, well, it will only make them angry). I don't recommend spraying a vampire, or a Wendigo with pepper spray. It's most likely worse than doing it to a grizzly bear.

GUN

This is a nice option to have if you're into killing innocent creatures. Of course, if the monster isn't so innocent, well, that's another story. Regardless, I don't recommend carrying a gun while hunting monsters – it will only make things worse. Unless of course it's a water gun filled with Holy Water and a touch of minced garlic.

BAGS

Seems silly to mention, but you should have some gallon-sized airtight freezer bags to bring specimens (hair, feces, bones, etc.) back to your lab (a.k.a garage) to analyze (sniff, taste, and poke at). They are also good for hauling food on your camp out into the wilderness. Just don't get the two confused. I'm thinking you don't want to eat any monster specimens, and it would be embarrassing to bring a turkey sandwich to the lab for analysis.

FIRST AID KIT

This is a must. Not only for aiding you after a monster attack, but more importantly for patching you up after running around in the dark, or walking into a tree while your night-vision goggles go on the blink.

HEADSET OR 2-WAY RADIO COMMUNICATIONS

Great to have for communicating between team members (Remember? You hunt with a buddy, right?). It's critical to keep in contact with others out there looking for the beasts.

INFRARED THERMAL SCANNER

This device allows you to measure heat signatures, where a creature may be, or have been, but you can't see them in the darkness. Very expensive, however, so this item is definitely optional. I use something less expensive, but not nearly as accurate. It's called a heat seeker, which reads changes in ambient temperatures, signaling the changes with LEDs. An even cheaper option at night is to just use a high-powered flashlight to look through the forest.

CELL PHONE

More for an emergency, rather than anything (although there are some good games to play, in those quiet moments of monster hunting).

MOTION DETECTORS

These devices detect motion, and are great for monitoring if people walk into a location, or to wake you up if a monster has wandered by. I suggest not placing them inside your tent unless you are a very still sleeper.

NIGHT VISION EQUIPMENT

This equipment is great for seeing monsters at night, with the normal lights off. Infrared lights are used (on the less expensive devices), which are invisible to the naked eye. But I've often wondered if the monster can see them.

NOTEBOOK/PENCIL

A small pad of paper and a pen is instrumental during the initial monster hunt. But a digital recorder in my opinion works just as well. As long as you have some way to keep track of your notes.

WRISTWATCH

Critical piece of equipment to make sure you keep on track during your investigation and to record the time when you stumble on the unusual and mysterious events. It's also good to have a watch with an alarm, in case you end up dozing while waiting for the monsters to appear.

As you can tell, there are a lot of things you can bring on a monster hunt. But the main thing is your brain. Think clearly about what you're doing. Safety is key. And always go with a team—never do it alone. (Okay, I admit it; I went alone on my Wendigo hunt, and I doubt I'll ever do that again!) Other safe things to do, is to remember that there can be other non-monster creatures out there, like bears, coyotes, and Chuck Norris, martial arts king. You don't want to surprise any of them, especially a Texas Ranger like Chuck Norris.

Another safety issue is to create a trip plan, specifying the time and location of where you're going. This can then be given to a friend, or somebody not going on the trip. Then, in case you don't return at the right time, the friend can notify the authorities that there may be a problem. Just don't give it to someone that's going with you, as they will most likely be in the same trouble you are.

Let's discuss the various techniques involved with monster hunting. The basic idea is to track monsters just like you would an animal. Keep an eye on the ground, as well as the air (especially if you're hunting a Mothman). Footprints tend to be one of the more common ways to provide evidence, second to pictures or video.

Really, the best way to track a monster is to use all six of your senses. The first five—sight, hearing, touch, smell, and taste, are commonly used in our daily lives. They can also be relied upon when finding monsters, although I'm thinking taste may be a tough one to swallow (unless you're hunting monster chocolate bunnies). Tasting a monster doesn't sound that safe, not to mention touching one.

The sixth sense, insight, or intuition, can be used as well. Especially when you're trying to cover hundreds of acres of forest. Sometimes, the best way to find the creature, is to relax for a moment, and focus on the beast, while observing the woods around you. When you get that notion of something happening in one location or another, go with it. That's your intuition. Of course, it may be telling you to go home, as only a crazy fool would be out in the woods at night searching for monsters, right?

I don't recommend forcing a monster out of its habitat. It will only make it mad, and I'm pretty sure you don't want to deal with a mad, angry monster. Although a happy monster is probably still nothing to handle lightly. And setting traps for the beasts of the night would be inappropriate as well. Sure, you may in fact catch the creature, but then what? I suppose you could take several pictures, then run like a bat out of hell as the monster breaks free.

I'm thinking your best bet to capture proof is to find evidence after the fact, to locate footprints, hair, feces, etc. It's much safer at least. Still, if you're fortunate enough to come face to face with a monster, don't just stand there, take pictures! Okay, you may want to run away while doing so, depending on how bad its breath is, and how hungry it looks.

Medusa, with snakes instead of hair, able to turn you into stone if you gaze upon her eyes, except of course when looking at a picture, right? Right? Hello?

As I've said, you want to look for signs of the creature, at a minimum. But it's also important where to look. For example, you probably don't need to look for Bigfoot in your bathtub, or anywhere in your house for that matter. Chances are, Bigfoot is up north in a forest somewhere, comfortably resting in his newly made nest of grass and branches. But where—which forest?

The best place to look is always wherever the monster was last sighted. Trying to find the creature in a place where it hasn't been seen for seventy-five years is as good as looking in your bathtub (or close to it). I'm not saying the monster will never be back to that location, but the likelihood is less than where it was more currently spotted.

And the timing of when you go hunting can be critical. Searching for Minnesota lake monsters in January would not be the most opportunistic time. Or honestly, trying to find a Wendigo in August, during the hot summer months, may not be appropriate. Wendigos (as you'll note after doing research), typically appear in winter months. It's important then, to do the appropriate research, to better understand your monster.

Lastly, make sure you report your findings. Keep track of them, by date, location, and description of what you've found. The more we track reports, the better we can get in finding a pattern to the monsters. Perhaps they are migratory, traveling from one location in the country to the next. That may help to pinpoint where and when to do your next hunt. Perhaps we can get a website put together, for all to enter their data into. That may give the monster hunting industry a big boost. And wouldn't it be great to find one of the monsters? To finally have major proof, to perhaps even acknowledge worldwide that monsters are real. What then? Will we be seeing them walking into your local Target store? Perhaps. But then that makes me wonder what they would buy. Hair removal products no doubt.

Hopefully you will enjoy the following stories. As I have indicated before, the story section in each chapter is based on true events. I've taken the liberty to combine them into one story, to tell (in a deep booming voice) around a campfire, to engage those on the fence about whether monsters are real. Perhaps the stories will ignite the monstrous fire within them, in a way in which they are excited to find out more. Then they can add to the adventure, possibly finding more evidence that monsters are out there. I also hope you enjoy the history sections, as they are exactly what I have found while doing my research. And a few chapters have my own field trips, where I went out to find the monster myself. That, in my opinion, was worth its weight in gold. The thrill and excitement of chasing monsters in the dark, is monstrous indeed.

BIG CATS OF BLOOMINGTON

"By heaven, he echoes me, as if there were some monster in his thought too hideous to be shown."

– William Shakespeare
English Dramatist, Playwright and Poet, 1564-1616

Forty years I've worked along the Minnesota River Valley in Port Cargill, just south of Bloomington, and I ain't never seen something so strange and scary.

Dead deer. At least a dozen of them. *Everywhere.* It was like a wicked mass murderer on the loose, escaped from Stillwater, killing bucks and does, with blood and guts everywhere—including on my snow boots.

I have to say, it scared the bajeezus out of me. Especially since I found it in the dead of night. As a night watchman, patrolling the area for the company I work for, I spend a lot of time walking through these woods. I only have to keep track of a few hundred acres, much easier than the thousands of wooded acres along the rest of the river banks. I make sure there's no trespassers, like teenagers having a secluded drinking party, or guys trying to fish from that perfect but private bend in the river, or farmers stealing grain out of the company's storage towers. But nobody warned me there would be monsters on the loose, killing deer and who knows what else. *Was I next?*

A light dusting of snow had fallen the night before, covering most of the deer carcasses. That meant whatever was attacking the poor defenseless deer, had been doing it for awhile. What alarmed me most, though, was that several deer were freshly killed, with no snow on them. In fact, the one shredded to pieces in front of me, was still warm.

The monster was not far away.

I instinctively reached for my gun, then quickly remembered as my hand dropped to my side, that I wasn't carrying one. Company policy. Nimrods. *How was I suppose to protect myself? Don't they know there's monsters in the woods!* The only weapon I had was a night stick, a long 4 D-cell battery flashlight, and I suppose my own blood curdling screaming ability.

I stood up, nervously checking that my flashlight was still working, and peered into the darkness. The snow-covered landscape, barren of vegetation, seemed to dampen all noise, with the cold winter night keeping things abnormally quiet.

A black jaguar, looking rather hungry.

I could hear the river in the distance, the ice crackling from on top while the water roared by underneath. I could hear in the distance the low rumble of late night trucks on Highway 13 and Interstate 35W. And I could hear the crunching snow of footsteps nearby. *Footsteps?*

I quickly swung my flashlight around, pointing it in the direction of the sound, but with the January sub-zero temperatures and my lack of decent gloves, the flashlight fell from my hands. After twirling several times, flashing at me like a primitive disco ball, the light landed in the snow and switched off, leaving me in total darkness. Well, except for the moonlight, stars, and the beady green eyes staring back at me.

Startled, I briefly used my blood curdling screaming abilities (more of a yelp than anything, though), before collecting myself together enough to do the only thing left—run. But what chance did I have to outrun a monster? Unless perhaps it was a sloth monster. No, I was most likely dead meat, soon to be a man among deer, a dead man among dead deer to be exact. Oh *deer* me.

Thankfully, I was a sprinter in high school, specializing in the hurdles. Sadly, that was over forty years ago, and I showed it. And running in the dark didn't help much either. It would have been faster if I'd just tried walking around the fallen trees and frozen swampy puddles. Instead, I tried leaping over them, like Carl Lewis in the Olympics. Of course, I ain't Lewis, and this wasn't the Olympics. I wondered briefly (very briefly) if that's how Mr. Lewis trained—having a green-eyed monster chase him in the dark.

I ended up mostly in the swampy slippery ice puddles. Or rather on them— flat out on my back. Or I was hugging fallen trees, like a deprived lumberjack stuck in the Sahara Desert for half a lifetime. Still, no monster caught up with me. Which, when getting back to the safety of my car, made me wonder, *Was I imagining things?* But I looked to my boots; the tips and sides were still covered with bloody snow.

"You look like you've seen a ghost!" exclaimed a voice from outside my car, after tapping on the side window of my now-running Chevy. My panting had frosted the windows, making it difficult to see in or out. At first I was startled, not being sure if my green-eyed monster was now standing tall and talking to me. Of course, if that were the case, it would have said something like, "I'm going to eat you!" or "Snack time!" Come to think of it, I'm sure the monster would just punch through the window, pull me out, and drag me back to his feasting throne.

"Kev? You okay?" asked the voice again. I rubbed the frost away to see my partner, Roger, standing there frowning. "You been drinking again?"

I shook my head while rolling down the window. It had been years since I nipped at the bottle. Well, at least while on duty. "I think I… I dunno. Something in the woods."

Roger stood back, centering his short, obese frame more evenly on his stocky legs. I could see his breath curling up into the cold, dry air. He tugged at his icicle-infested mustache and chuckled. "You afraid of the boogeyman?"

I shrugged my shoulders. "Dunno. Maybe. But I have proof. Dead deer everywhere." I pointed back to the woods. "There's something out there, Roger, with green eyes."

Roger looked into the woods. It wasn't as intimidating, being I was now in a parking lot, sitting in a running car, with my foot ready on the accelerator, if need be. Roger waved his hand. "Come on, let's go take a look then."

"You nuts?" I said in a squeaky voice. "I'm not going back there at night ever again."

Roger thought for a moment while pulling more icicles off his mustache. "Tell you what. You know those trail cameras we use when deer hunting? Let's set one up tomorrow. We'll go in broad daylight. Both of us."

I nodded with approval. "But I'm bringing my shotgun."

"Works for me," said Roger, then turned to me with his arms raised and yelled, "Boo!"

I nearly wet my pants, which is never a good thing in a frigid Minnesota winter. Mad, I yelled at Roger, "You can finish the shift without me!" I rolled the window up and went home, the whole way looking repeatedly in my rear view mirror (and back seat), to make sure there were no green-eyed monsters following me.

The next night I waited an hour for Roger to show, standing in the parking lot with my trail camera filled with fresh batteries. But he was nowhere to be found. I checked at work, and they had not seen him either. *Did the green-eyed monster get him?*

Getting impatient, I decided to head back to the deer carnage spot myself. Yeah, I know. Probably a dumb idea, and certainly not like me. But I had Betsy with me, my 12 gauge shotgun. Ain't nobody gonna mess with Betsy and me. Of course, I still wasn't sure what the monster was. Perhaps it had a gun, too?

After several minutes of walking through the woods, and lots of feeling like somebody (or something) was watching me, I cautiously entered the deer killing area, Betsy locked and loaded. Nothing had changed, other than another thin layer of snow had covered the deer.

Yet, once again, a fresh deer had been killed. By the looks of it, only an hour or two ago.

Hearing some rustling behind me, I swung around, finger pressed against the trigger; I could sense Betsy wanted some action. And if the movement was the green-eyed monster, she would get some.

"Whoa cowboy!" yelled a voice from the moving bushes. I lowered Betsy, seeing it was Roger. He was busy fixing his pants. "What kind of friend are you? Don't you know it's not nice to shoot people when they're taking a leak?"

"Sorry about that," I said. "I thought…"

"That I was a monster?" Roger sighed deeply. "Kevin, do you *really* think there's such things as monsters?" He shook his head. "Come on, look around you. This is all from some wild animal."

"But there's got to be a dozen dead dear here," I replied. "It's got to be something big. Or maybe a pack of wolves."

Roger laughed. "Kev, Kev, Kev. We're practically downtown Minneapolis, just a few miles away. Do you *think* there's a pack of wolves running around?" He pointed to some of the prints in the snow. "Look here. This is probably some big cat. A lynx, or something."

"One lynx is doing all this killing?" I shook my head. "Doubtful."

"We'll find out soon enough," said Roger as he pointed to a nearby tree. "That camera there will give us proof. With the motion sensor and infrared light, we'll catch your monster, eventually." He reached for the trail camera I brought. "Let's put yours up on the other side."

Three days went by before we caught something on the cameras. Until then I have to tell you it was a bit nerve-racking having to patrol the woods at night. But, even though it was against policy, I had Betsy with me. Roger, too. But my odds for safety weighed more heavily on Betsy and her gunpowder authority.

We were alert to even the most minuscule movement and sounds coming from the wooded darkness. Although our attentive attitude might also have had something to do with the four Red Bulls we drank beforehand. Or maybe because at any moment, we wondered if in fact there was a green-eyed monster stalking us, watching our every move, waiting for the right time to attack.

Most of the pictures on the camera were of deer (live ones), a few raccoons, and the occasional hawk. But on the third day of checking, we hit pay dirt. There, hunched over a freshly killed deer, tearing into its shoulder, was a big black cat. No, not your typical cuddly house cat. This thing was huge, about the size of a German Sheppard. One picture we caught had the monster cat staring at us, as if in defiance; its green eyes glowing in the infrared image.

"I can feel it," said Roger as we tromped through the crunchy January snow in the dark, away from our parked cars. "You hear it?"

"Hear what?" I asked, perplexed.

Roger stopped moving and tilted his head to the clear, star-twinkling sky. "I can hear nothing." He continued walking to the deer kill area. "They say, when you don't hear anything at all in the woods, there's a predator out there, waiting, stalking you."

I wondered who "they" were, and where Roger came up with the idea. Either way, I think he was right. I could feel it, too. Things were a bit too quiet. There was some comfort in knowing what the monster was. Still, a large, deer-eating cat kept me on edge. If it could take down a couple hundred-pound deer, it could take down a slow-moving beer-belly guy like me. For sure. I began to wonder if in fact Betsy would protect me. *Would I point and shoot fast enough?* I looked up high. *Would the cat jump us from the trees?*

"Watch where you're pointing that!" Roger gently pushed Betsy out of his way.

"Right," I said, nervously setting Betsy up on my shoulder. "The cat," I added, while my eyes darted back and forth, "could be any-where."

"And probably up by those dead deer," said Roger, pointing ahead. "There's the place. Let's see if there's any new tracks."

Roger seemed excited about finding this big black cat. I wasn't. I don't think he's done the research. There shouldn't be any large cats in Minnesota, especially a dozen miles from downtown Minneapolis. And a cat that size could jump on you and slash your throat in less than a second. They're natural born killers. I, on the other hand, was a natural born wimp.

Both of us walked over to a freshly killed deer. We kneeled next to it, spooked out by the carnage. There was blood drenched snow everywhere.

Roger bent over closer to it, staring at its chest. "I think… this one's still breathing." Just then, the hind leg of the downed deer kicked, grazing the side of me, sending me falling backward. Which also sent Betsy to the ground, dropping into the snow. Not good. Especially when we heard the crack of a twig nearby.

"Did you hear something?" asked Roger. We both looked behind us. "Over there?"

Another crackling sound.

Before I knew what happened, it was over.

In a blur, I saw the big cat leap at us. Perhaps it was protecting its recent venison snack, or maybe we were its next meal. But the cat, after an explosion of gunfire, was no more.

"You two okay?" came a voice from the bushes. Several police officers came running out.

I looked at them, then at the dead cougar inches from me. "I'm okay. But I don't think the cat is."

I've retired from patrolling the woods, but I'll never forget that night. Both Roger and I would surely have been dead, mauled to shreds by the big cougar, if it weren't for the Bloomington Police Department. They had heard about the big cat too, and were stalking it as well. I don't go on walks at night anymore, not unless I'm walking with Betsy.

HISTORY

TWIT (TUNE WHILE I TYPE)

BLACK DOG BY LED ZEPPELIN

When I first heard about this story, that it happened in Bloomington, I shivered at the thought. Why? Because I lived in Bloomington back in the 90s when this happened, and not too far from the location. And to think, I could have been out on a walk late at night, and could've gotten mauled by a giant cat.

What kind of cat you ask? According to the police report, it was a black cougar. They once roamed North America from the snow-capped mountains of Alaska to the heated Tierra del Fuego. That, of course, was over a hundred years ago. So why would a cougar show up now? Are they coming back into population again? Possibly.

There have been many sightings of big cats throughout the state, but they are usually just stories people tell. With the story in the beginning of this chapter, we have proof. We have pictures. As the story indicates, the man, Mr. Kammann, used his trail camera to take pictures of the beast, in the dead of night near Port Cargill south of Bloomington.

He had heard rumors about the creature, and couldn't believe it. To find out for sure, he used his motion sensor infrared camera, mounted on a tree, to take pictures near the area where the deer hides and bones were found. Sure enough, within a few days, he had the proof.

A large mountain lion, similar to ones
that are apparently starting to appear
around the Midwest once again.

The pictures clearly showed a cougar, also known as a mountain lion, puma, or panther. He also saw scratch marks on a nearby tree from the beast, carved into the bark up four feet high. It was a big one to say the least. Similar to the female cougar shot near Big Sandy Lake, weighing in well over fifty pounds.

The question most people have is whether the big cat was wild, or possibly a pet. Perhaps it was wild, traveling through the area from Montana or the Black Hills, on its way to somewhere deep in the forests around Wisconsin Dells. There would be plenty of food for it, like deer, fox, rabbits; quite the Meow Mix. And of course, what's more concerning, is if it would prey upon our pet cats, or dogs, or even children. Alarming indeed.

A female cougar's territory can cover up to thirty-six square miles of a forest, with a male cat ten times more than that. On the one hand, that's reassuring, if you live in a more densely populated area. It would be difficult for a large cat like a cougar to survive. Or is it? If it were able to remain stealthy, it could feed at night on stray animals, or in dumpsters. Still, one would think that if there were an abundance of the creatures, there would be even more stories heard, and more pictures taken.

But a cougar, in the rural areas of Minnesota, could possibly be real. Even an area only ten miles from downtown Minneapolis, such as Bloomington, might support the big cat. The area along the Minnesota river, is heavily forested, with part of it known as the Minnesota Valley National Wildlife Refuge. Perhaps even the big cats are taking part in the refuge. With over 14,000 acres in the refuge alone, not to mention the forested area spreading from St. Paul to Mankato, there is ample space to sustain a big, black cougar. And maybe even a family of them.

Just down from where the cougar was spotted in Port Cargill, another man reported finding tracks after a fresh snowfall, the size of burgers, near a local quarry. The news wouldn't have been much different than what was found by Mr. Kammann, except for the fact that multiple prints were found, some slightly smaller than the others. Could this be a family of cougars living in the area? Possibly.

There have been other sightings of big cats around the state, like the one reported at a state park. A man had just finished pitching his tent, to settle in for a nice quiet sleep, but was awaken to the sounds of low, full-throated screaming. It didn't sound like coyotes, much deeper and crazier than that. Turns out in his case, a large, black panther had recently escaped from a nearby house.

Many sightings can apparently be attributed to large house cats. One in particular, the Maine Coon, can sometimes be over 25" long, weighing over 20 pounds. The largest in fact was well over 3 feet long. While the larger house cats are big (I myself have a Norwegian Forest cat over 20" long), I can't imagine anyone being that confused by them, especially when a big black cougar could easily weigh in over 100 pounds. Still, from a distance, and in the dusk or dawn when these cats are usually seen, looks could in fact be deceiving.

Another big cat was spotted in Willmar, Minnesota, wandering around town near Kennedy Elementary School. The Wildcat Sanctuary of Cedar, Minnesota, eventually picked the cat up, to take it to Chicago (and from there to a sanctuary down south). But it wasn't your basic house cat. In this case, it was in fact a cougar.

Where it came from is still a mystery. This big cat made national news, astounding the country and wondering how a cougar could be found roaming freely through the streets of a city. Needless to say, the students in the elementary school stayed indoors until the big cat was captured. But I'm sure there were many wide-eyed looks from the windows as the beast strolled by.

In December 2009, reports came in that a large cat was spotted in the Champlin area, just north of Brooklyn Park. Video captured the large cougar meandering across Highway 169. As of this writing, the cougar has not been caught. The DNR estimate (based on video footage) the cougar to weigh 200 pounds.

One of my favorite shows, *Monsterquest*, had an episode on big cats called, "Lions in the Backyard." They claim that some of the reasons for the cougars entering our towns and cities have to do with urban sprawl. More and more housing developments are pushing their way into the forests and natural habitats of the cats. With that, there have been hundreds of big black cat sightings across the country, some estimated at six feet long and weighing over 250 pounds.

So what is the likelihood of a big cat showing up in your backyard? Well, there are 10,000 to 30,000 big cats in North America. It's doubtful there are that many in Minnesota, but the possibility is there. Which makes you wonder how safe it may be to ride your bike late at night, or take a walk after the sun has set. But only out in rural areas, right? Wrong.

In 1999, in Hugo, Minnesota, only thirty miles north of Minneapolis, a black cat was reported by David Johnson. It was as long as a German Shepherd (four feet in length), with a slender, muscular build, and large paws. Mr. Johnson not only reported the incident, but was also able to take pictures, providing even more evidence that the creatures do find their way into more populated areas.

While it's easy to assume that the sightings and captures of the cougars come from somebody's loose pet, not all of them can be explained that easily. In some cases, large, 250 pound lamas were attacked, and other large animals as well, such as horses (perhaps explaining some of the cattle mutilations occasionally reported). Some say there could be jaguars on the loose, or even a lion, tiger, or puma. Yet, historically there has never been a report of something that large in Minnesota.

And in October of 2009, there was a report of a large cat from Lanesboro, Minnesota, southwest of Rochester. Several horses were attacked (closer to Preston), clawed to death by an unknown animal. One horse was never found. Finding your horse clawed and half-eaten is one thing, as it is difficult to pinpoint what animal did it (other than a rather large one). But the man from Lanesboro, through the use of his trail camera, captured several pictures of a large cat. Many in the area believe it to be a cougar, perhaps over seventy pounds. I've looked at the pictures, and it does appear to be some type of large cat. Which makes me think twice about walking the dogs late at night anymore.

Perhaps there are some rogue big cats showing up, feeding on deer and other animals in the night. That is one thing. Hopefully it's nothing more than that. There are reports in 2007 about the Beast of Exmoor in England – a black feline, pointy ears, long tail – seven feet long nose to tail. So maybe the next time you're letting out the dog in the backyard for a late night bathroom break, keep an eye on them. Or that early morning peaceful jog into the country – make sure you are not being followed by a big black cat. And just in case, don't hesitate to carry along an industrial-sized bag of Meow Mix – it may just save your life.

Fieldtrip

My plan was to head up to Port Cargill and do an investigation of my own. Perhaps I could still find some big paw prints in the mud along the Minnesota River, camping out for a few days until a cat showed up. But I didn't have a gun, and wasn't too sure I wanted to get eaten by a big black cougar. Still, it wouldn't hurt to check things out a bit.

After driving around the area for awhile, I concluded there was no easy way to gain access to the area (other than tromping through the forest on the wet, murky day). Every turn I took I was confronted with a "No Trespassing" sign. I briefly thought about sneaking in to have a look around, but thought otherwise. Perhaps the sign was there for a reason, like keeping people from walking around and getting eaten by a cougar. I decided not to take any chances, so ended up just taking a few pictures from the edge of the forest, and studied the area for a while. After several drives along the perimeter, I concluded it was a large enough area for a cougar to hide in.

The place seemed eerie and desolate, covered mostly by a forest, with only the nearby grain elevators rising up into the sky. It seemed like I was in the middle of nowhere when I looked into the wooded land. Yet, only a few blocks away was busy Highway 13, and only a couple miles away were Interstate 35 on one side and Highway 169 on the other. Overall, the place was surrounded by civilization, but inside the refuge area, was a wilderness teeming with an ample food supply to support a big cat—perhaps even several of them.

Artist's rendition of the elusive
Bigfoot creature, depicting the
typical hairy body, ape-like face,
and, well, big feet.

BIGFOOT OF TWO HARBORS

"Is it better to out-monster the monster or to be quietly devoured?"

— *Friedrich Nietzsche*

There's so many stories about Bigfoot. Or Sasquatch, big hairy ape-man, Yeti… you name it. But they're just stories, right? Well, I use to think they were, but ever since moving to Northern Minnesota, I've changed my mind. Bigfoot is real. Very real.

It all started back in the late 1980s, at my cabin just north of Two Harbors. God's Country, as I like to call it. The North Shore of Lake Superior is one of the most beautiful and pristine areas of the country, in my opinion, if not the world. I can think of no better place to live. And I suppose Bigfoot has the same idea.

We had just moved from the Buckeye State, Ohio, trying hard to settle into the hard life of the densely wooded landscape. There wasn't much to do – no nearby dance clubs, fast food, or movie theaters. And there wasn't much for jobs, since the ore and taconite mining dried up and went overseas. The economy wasn't much better in Ohio though, so the move seemed to make sense. I needed a change. Something different. *Something Bigfoot?*

The cabin, a few miles north of Two Harbors, a bit off National Forest Highway 15 and not too far from the North Shore Trail, was rustic to say the least. There was no electricity, no indoor plumbing, and no running water. It was basically a place to sleep… and party. Being in my younger twenties, staying up late with friends and watching a bonfire crackle and roar in the backyard was a priority. Apparently, that was Bigfoot's idea too.

I had a friend from Ohio over, sitting around the fire pit, chatting about typical things, like music, movies, and baseball. The Twins had just won the World Series. I wasn't a native Minnesotan, but I got into it all the same. Go Kirby Puckett! Eventually, however, the subject of spooky things came up.

"Do you believe in ghosts?" asked my friend Henry, to Wendy, one of the girls we'd met at the local pub in Two Harbors (and yes, our beer goggles were on). Henry was my best friend growing up in

Ohio, and I suppose was still my best friend. There wasn't many ways to meet people up north, unless you fished, hunted, or hiked. I wasn't much good at any of them… yet. But I was willing to learn. Especially if a certain girl from a local pub was willing to persuade me.

Wendy giggled nervously, shaking her head. "Yeah, right. For sure."

"There's no such things as that, Tom," replied the other girl, Samantha, to me as she gulped down another Schmidt, belching loudly with approval, sending a baritone echo deep into the surrounding forest. My kind of girl. Any woman who can belch like that has to be good for something.

Henry, the veritable jokester and drama king, started in on a ghost story, filled with haunting details. Before long the girls were inched up closer to us, quietly sitting wide-eyed on the edge of their chairs. And of course, at the most opportunistic moment, the climax of the story, Henry screamed. The girls shrieked, echoing his (only in a much higher octave), then flopped back in their chairs with their hands hiding their faces. As if that would save them from a ghost.

Henry and I laughed. That is until we heard the high-pitched shrieking not too far in the distant darkness.

"What the—" said Henry, standing up, tipping back his chair and peering into the black forest beyond the fire. "You hear that?"

"Yeah," I replied, swallowing hard. I'd never heard anything like that. Not in Ohio. Not since I moved here. The shrieking returned; this time more of a howling.

And it sounded closer.

"Ha, ha," said Samantha, punching me hard in the shoulder. "Not funny." She turned to the darkness and yelled. "Come on out, whoever you are." She turned back to me, punching my shoulder again. "Who's your howling friend out there?"

I wish it was a friend of mine. This would have been a great joke, a way to get the girls closer and more intimate. But it wasn't any plan of mine. I looked over at Henry, who was just as perplexed as I was. He shrugged his shoulders, then took another sip of beer.

But the howling became growling.

"That doesn't sound good," I said, with a feeble attempt at chuckling. All of us, now standing, took a closer step to the fire. Which was worse – being burned to death by a bonfire, or eaten by some strange creature of the night?

"Perhaps we should go inside?" squeaked Henry. His voice was so high, I thought it was Wendy's at first.

We all agreed that was the best thing to do, as the sounds seemed to be coming from just outside the light of the bonfire. Led by me and my trusty lantern, we quickly moved into the cabin.

As we peered out the window toward the dying fire, shining my flashlight back and forth, we could see something moving and growling, swiftly darting around the edge of the fire. It was dark, tall, and not so handsome. From what I could tell, it stood at least seven feet tall, and was covered in thick, black hair. It was too dark outside to see what the face looked like, but the glowing eyes twinkled now and then in the fire and flashlight. The growling continued for quite some time, until at last the fire was reduced to embers, and my battery power on the flashlight was getting low.

I have to say, I was terrified. I was mostly worried that whatever was out there, would come in the cabin. Why wouldn't it? Why hadn't it done so already? Or maybe, with the silence now blanketing the dimly lit area outside (not a creature was stirring), the monster *was* inside.

Nervously shining the flashlight around the room, from one person to the next, I slowly relaxed, counting only the five of us. Five? There were only supposed to be four of us! Now it was my turn for a alto-soprano shriek.

"Monster!" I yelled, pointing to the dark mass behind us.

Henry turned, then laughed. "Ha! That's no monster." He walked over and reached at the thing, only to reveal his jacket on the coat hook near the door. "Man, you're really freaked out. Look, whatever was out there, was just some type of animal. No big deal."

"A seven-foot-tall animal?" I snapped while still searching the room with my flashlight, which was now hardly emanating any type of light.

"Let's just relax and enjoy the rest of the night," said Henry while putting his arm around Wendy. "Let's have another beer."

All of us agreed a beer would be good about now, except there was a slight problem: The beer was in the cooler, out by the dead fire. Not good.

Henry and I spent the next few minutes reenacting an argument between the Skipper and Gilligan from *Gilligan's Island*. Or maybe Drake and Josh from Nickelodeon's *Drake & Josh Show*. We went back and forth with, "I'm not going out there, you go out there..."

Finally, we decided both of us should go get the cooler. After all, we were men, right? No silly seven-foot-tall-hulking-black-wild animal's gonna scare us. Yeah, right. But we had women in here to protect, and to show off our macho manliness. So we armed ourselves as best we could; I had a hammer, Henry found a small, stubby screwdriver.

I shook my head. "What are you going to do with a screwdriver? Poke the monster to death?"

Henry made sharp stabbing motions, about head level. "I'll gouge his eyes out."

"Good luck with that," I said. "I'm sure it'll just stand there and let you do it."

"But you'll be hitting it with the hammer. Or are you going out to repair the barn?"

"Very funny," I said as we opened the squeaky cabin door. Man,

I never knew how loud a squeaky door could be. It must have echoed a mile away, probably signaling for the monster to come back for a snack, if in fact it had left at all.

Side by side, we slowly shuffled our way over to the other side of the glowing embers, now barely visible, to the cooler full of our much-needed treasure. But was it worth it? To get mauled by a monster over a Schmidt beer? Maybe.

"Where's the cooler?" asked Henry, looking around.

"There… and there… and there… everywhere," I said. Something had smashed the flimsy Styrofoam cooler to bits, spreading beer cans and ice across the area.

"I guess the monster wanted a beer too," said Henry.

Growling and thrashing came from the woods nearby.

"Correction," I squeaked. "It *wants* beer." I started picking up cans of beer from the ground. "Come on, grab a few and let's get back in the cabin!"

It seemed as though the monster wanted desperately to thwart our plans. I don't know if it wanted the beers, or us. Most likely both.

What happened next was one of those scenes you replay in your head for the rest of your life, looking back on it and laughing. At the moment, however, it was horrific. Henry, a much faster runner than I, was several steps ahead of me… and the monster Bigfoot. I say Bigfoot now, because I could clearly see the huge hulking bipedal monster, with its flared nostrils, thin lips, and glaring eyes.

Bigfoot was coming at us, but more me then Henry. In a valiant effort, Henry began wasting the precious beers, throwing them at Bigfoot, hoping I suppose to either scare it off, or lure him away by the succulent carbonated beverages. Neither worked, and Bigfoot was within a few feet of me.

It was at this point I realized just how big the creature was, at least two feet taller than me, and several times wider. And he stunk worse than a week-old road-kill deer on the side of Interstate 35 in July. But that was the least of my worries. I also quickly realized my weapon was gone, having dropped the hammer while sprinting to safety. But just as soon as I thought I was dead meat, to be eaten alive by a terrorized ape-like creature, Bigfoot was gone. It passed between us, continuing its way into the woods, never to be seen again… sort of.

Several times over the next few years, we encountered the large, furry, curious creature, before eventually moving back home to Ohio. To this day I don't know if he was looking for a party, or to drink beer, or just play with the shiny cylindrical objects. I don't think he meant any harm, though. Every time he's shown up, he's trying to run away more than anything. But perhaps that's because I switched from Schmidt beer to Old Milwaukee. He could possibly have a thing for the finer pleasures of Minnesota, rather than Wisconsin…

HISTORY

TWIT (TUNE WHILE I TYPE)
WITCH HUNT BY RUSH

This, of course, is probably one of the most well-known monsters studied. If you haven't heard of Bigfoot, you've been living under a rock in the middle of nowhere. Of course Bigfoot might be there too.

The story above focuses on a man living just outside of Two Harbors, who had repeated visits by Bigfoot, (or some type of Bigfoot creature), over several years. As for me, I'm not sure I would have stuck around after the first sighting. Especially since the creature was bold enough to visit their campfire so close. But perhaps Bigfoot was just lonely, wanting to partake in the festivities. Doubtful.

Bigfoot, with its hundreds of sightings over the years, apparently spans coast to coast on the northern side of the country, and up into Canada (although in Canada, it's referred to as Sasquatch quite frequently). And it's not just North America that has these creatures inhabiting it. The Himalayas have a Bigfoot creature called Yeti.

Although most people have a good idea what the creature looks like (especially if you've seen the famous Patterson film from the 60s), I thought I should describe to you, in general, what the creature looks like. At a high level, Bigfoot is a tall, heavy, hairy, gorilla-like creature that walks upright on two legs. It's typically reported as being around seven feet tall, with broad, hairy shoulders, a gorilla-like face with flaring nostrils and big brown eyes. It is thought that the creature is a herbivore, wanting to only eat nuts and berries. To date, there are no reports of Bigfoot eating animals, or people for that matter. That is to say that anyone that has been eaten by Bigfoot has not reported the incident.

And you might wonder just how many sightings have been reported in Minnesota? A ton of them. To give you an example, below is a list of sightings collected by Joseph Heinan on his Minnesota Bigfoot website: www.angelfire.com/mn2/mnbf/.

North of Hawley, Minnesota, October 1995

Hugo, Minnesota, Winter 1978

Ely, Minnesota, November 2000

Shakopee, Minnesota, early 60s & 70s

Brainerd, Minnesota, April 1974

Northern Minnesota, (no precise location given),
early 90s

White Earth, Minnesota, 1970s

**Gravel road near Strawberry Lake in Becker County,
Minnesota,** July 2000

North McDougal Lake near Isabella, Minnesota,
(no date given)

Few miles south of Carlton, Minnesota, July 4, 2002
around 10 pm

Near Northome, Minnesota, 1970s (Middle of the night)

Near Ely, Minnesota, January 1997

**Sherburne National Wildlife Refuge Near Blue Hill
and Zimmerman, Minnesota,** November 1998

Forty miles west of St. Croix River, date not specified

Town Hall Road north of Bemidji, Minnesota,
July 2001

Near Mcgregor, Minnesota, November 1999

Thirteen miles west of Togo, Minnesota,
August 5, 2003

Near Frontenac State Part In Goodhue County,
Early 1970s

Highway 53 Near Cotton and Canyon, Minnesota,
September 7, 2004 around 7:20 a.m.

As you can tell, there are many sightings, spanning decades. There was one reported on October 24th 2009 in Bemidji. A trail camera even captured a picture of the monster as it walked past, with its thick, black hair gleaming in the darkness.

What's more interesting to me, is that the sightings are not necessarily just up in northern Minnesota. There are some further south, and not too far from where I live in Rochester. Yikes! I guess it goes to show that the big, hairy creature doesn't always need a thick, dense forest to live in. Or maybe it was visiting his friend the Mothman (see the Mothman chapter in this book), or his giants living in Chatfield.

But how can such a gigantic monster elude us so easily? I mean, after decades of sightings, we've never caught one, or captured that perfect picture, or have one appear on *Oprah*. The typical answer is that the creature is essentially nocturnal and shy, keeping to itself. Still, I would think we'd find huts or nests or burrows that it lived in, not to mention Bigfoot dung.

Another theory to its elusiveness has to do with the ability to transport itself from place to place via an alternate dimension. Yeah, right. While I like the idea of that being possible (and wouldn't mind using that as I write this on a plane traveling from Phoenix to Minneapolis), I highly doubt it's a reality. But let's say it's true—Bigfoot is a multi-dimensional being. And we, in our singular 3D-plus-time lifeline expect to catch one? Good luck with that endeavor. Let's just say that the creature would be in the category of Aliens, being way far advanced from our state of existence. It would be like finding a microscopic needle in a haystack the size of Toledo.

Regardless of your beliefs on how the creature lives (or if it lives at all), we must remember that in the end, there are people seeing something. While it has become difficult to solve the mystery, one has to admit that there's something out there. Perhaps all of us who are avid campers, could do a little investigating, setting up a camera or two in the middle of the night. Then maybe, we'd find the proof we need. We could then move forward living in harmony with the Bigfoot – Sasquatch – Yeti creature. That is, of course, provided it doesn't want to eat us.

FIELDTRIP

Okay. I'm thinking, of all the investigations I should go on, hunting for Bigfoot has to be at the top of the list. My original plan had me hunting for it just north of Two Harbors on Friday the 13th. Pretty cool, huh? Well, the planets didn't align, and I had other commitments. Darn. Nothing like hunting monsters on Mr. Badluck Day Friday the 13th. The only thing worse would be hunting on Saturday the 14th. Which is, in fact, what I did. Er, wanted to that is. At least that was the plan. But once again, "other" things became a priority (yes, there's more to life than hunting monsters, or at least that's what my wife says). Eventually, I did go monster hunting for Bigfoot, but not until late November – during Thanksgiving weekend. There's nothing wrong with that—I was hoping to be thankful, coming back alive, that is.

An interestingly deep gauge found on a tree four feet up, while searching for Bigfoot. Could it be the beast marking its territory?

Being that I'm writing this book, I obviously made it back just fine. The four hour trip up Interstate 35 north to Two Harbors turned out to be a blast. My brother, Erik, who is also a writer and fascinated with the unknown (like when the next book of his will be on the best-seller's list). I packed up all my gear (picture camera, thermal heat seeking device, video camera, trail camera, digital audio recorder, headlamp, and a multitude of Monster energy drinks). I even brought along plaster, for making footprint molds, just in case we found some interesting and unusual ones.

Like everything else in life, we were racing to get it done. The sun was setting at 4:21p.m. in Two Harbors that time of year, and as I suspected, the GPS Navigator indicated we would be in Two Harbors by 4:20 p.m. That would give us a whopping minute to get setup for the hunt. And as far as setting up tents and camping, that was not an option anymore. Mainly for two reasons: one was that it was getting too late – I hate setting up tents in the dark. And two, it was getting too cold (low 30s), where I not only hate setting up tents in the cold, I hate even more sleeping in them.

After the long haul on I-35, we picked up the 61 Expressway outside of Duluth, on our way to Two Harbors. Only Two Harbors wasn't the final stop. We needed to go north on County Highway 2 about fifteen miles, just past UT46, to hit the North Shore Trail. The location is a bit south of the Superior National Forest, where one would assume there's lots of places for Bigfoot to live and hide. Which probably helps build a solid story as to why there have been so many sightings in the area.

Thankfully, there was a full moon out, giving us a decent amount of light to work with (although I wasn't entirely sure we wouldn't meet up with a werewolf). We parked in the parking lot and suited up for the expedition. Our plan was to walk through the forest, mostly along the North Shore Trail, with night-vision cameras rolling. Eventually, we would find a location to setup the trail camera, and set out bait. The bait we used, good or bad, was oranges. We thought through the different options on bait, from hamburger to bananas (everyone likes a good burger or a sweet banana, regardless of species, right?). But in the end, we decided on oranges, giving Bigfoot a tropical paradise treat in the frigid temperatures, when compared to the typical nuts and berries it eats.

That is, of course, assuming it was a vegetarian. If it turned out to be a carnivore or omnivore, well, we were in big trouble. Especially since neither one of us had a gun. I did bring with us some pepper spray, which would work well on black bears, but for anything bigger it would probably just annoy it.

The other factor of danger, was that it was hunting season. We could hear in the distance gunshots, which didn't make us feel very welcome. It seemed that either way, we wouldn't be coming out of the woods alive. But we trekked on, anxious to find proof of Bigfoot. After about an hour, we came to a clearing, a split in the path – one direction continued along the North Shore Trail, the other was the Yukon Trail intersection. This seemed like a perfect spot for the trail camera.

We setup the camera without incident, although we had a lengthy debate on which way to point it. I concluded (since it was my camera) that we'd point it toward the wider area, down the North Shore Trail. And with the oranges sliced and set out in front, we moved on with our investigation.

The author (left) and his brother
(right) while hunting for Bigfoot
(not shown). Or is it the author and
Bigfoot hunting for his brother?

For the remainder of the night, we heard the occasional branch snapping, or possible shuffling in the weeds farther into the darkness, but never captured any evidence of Bigfoot. And being that it was too dark, we couldn't see much in the way of footprints. That would have to take place the next day, in daylight.

We also decided it would be appropriate to investigate a nearby cemetery, Lakeview Cemetery. We peacefully wandered among the tombstones, doing some EVP (Electronic Voice Phenomena) readings, and taking a few pictures. While it was an enjoyable experience, we didn't find anything of interest, other than one picture with an odd yellow light, possibly an electrifying orb of spiritual energy. But, since this book is about monsters, I won't get into further details about ghosts. Goblins, however, would be a different story.

The next day, after a fitful sleep, dreaming of large, hairy bipedal monsters terrorizing the town of Two Harbors, we went back up County Highway 2, to the North Shore Trail to retrieve the trail camera. This time while on the trail, we searched the ground for any possible Bigfoot prints. Unfortunately, we found none, but did find a large catlike paw print that seemed huge. Perhaps the big cat of Bloomington followed us here? Could be. It definitely made you think about all the wild animals that were living in the area. And was Bigfoot one of them?

We arrived at the site where the trail camera was setup, along with the orange bait, eager to see what had happened. Unfortunately, nothing had happened. The oranges were more or less in the same position I had left them. There were, however, several pictures taken by the trail camera. But they ended up (after reviewing them back at home) being nothing more than me setting up the trail camera, and me taking it down. So perhaps all it proved was that Bigfoot is not a herbivore. Or maybe he just didn't like the brand of oranges I bought at Rainbow Foods.

Regardless of the findings, it was well worth it to do our own Bigfoot investigation. Sure, it would have been great to find a footprint, using some plaster to capture it. Or to review the footage of our night-vision camera, to find Bigfoot smiling and waving at us from the bushes. Or the trail camera might have caught Bigfoot gorging himself on fresh Florida oranges. But none of that happened. What did happen, was me getting to experience the thrill and adventure of searching for the unknown. That, my friends, is always worth the risk of getting attacked by wild cougars or bears, or even Bigfoot, right?

Spooky troll, similar to ones
inhabiting a house in Cannon Falls.

DEMON TROLLS OF CANNON FALLS

"You never get used to waking up at night and finding a troll coming out of your closet…"

It first started when I was nine months old. I could see the thing through a mirror in my room as I stood at the end of the crib. I'll never forget how terrified I was, seeing the short little troll-like creature running around my room, with gnarled face, beady-red eyes, and razor-sharp finger nails. I screamed. My mother came in, but she could not see it. Still, the scream helped as the troll left the room. But not for long.

A few years had passed but my memory of the troll was as sharp as ever. I had just turned five years old, and could tell there was something strange going on in the house. I was sure the troll was back again. Footsteps in the middle of the night became a common occurrence. I could handle the footsteps; that didn't bother me. It was the beady-red eyes staring at me through the slats in my closet door.

The door to my closet had slats across it. I was told that lets the clothes in the closet breathe and stay fresh. What they didn't realize was that it let the trolls breathe too. And stare at me through the slats. I'll tell you right now, there's nothing more scary than waking up at night, having the feeling someone's watching you, only to roll over and see two beady-red eyes looking at you down low through your closet door. Well, there is one thing even scarier than that. Having those two beady-red eyes staring at you from alongside your bed is worse.

I would have been quite happy with the troll staying in the closet. Beady-red eyes and all. But they didn't stay there. One night I could hear something prancing around in the room, most likely walking from the closet to my bed, or over to the door to the hallway. The next night, I could tell something was pacing back and forth around my bed from one side to the other. I eventually got up enough nerve to open my eyes. I really don't recommend doing that. It's only going to terrify you.

Slowly opening my eyes, I peered across my bed toward the closet door. No beady-red eyes. Good. But I still had that feeling something was watching me. I looked down at the foot of my bed, not wanting to find anything. Thankfully, I didn't. Feeling a bit better, I rolled over opposite the closet door. Bad idea. That's when I saw it.

There's nothing like staring down a troll, point blank. It was inches from my face. I could feel its stinky breath on me. Its beady-red eyes framed around a gnarling leather-skinned face and wide grin stared at me, as if waiting for me to scream. I didn't disappoint it.

There are light, dainty screams, the kind you make when you're really not that scared, more just alarmed than anything. Then there's the heavy blood-curdling screams. That's what I yelled. It did the trick. In an instant, the troll was gone. My mom came rushing into the room, expecting to find me dead by the way I screamed. I told her about the troll. What surprised me even more was that she understood.

What I didn't realize was that my mom had her own incidents in the house. Big, tall, shadowy figures roaming from room to room. She could sense they were men, or at least were at one time. She had been visited many times by them, always terrified and never the same afterward. I never saw the tall shadow men; the trolls were enough for me.

I began to wonder if there was something about the house, or perhaps the location of it. The house had been around for over 100 years. It's located just off East Park in Cannon Falls. It doesn't seem like a house that would have a connection to other worlds. But it does. We had a psychic stop by and check things out at one point. She immediately knew there was a presence here. Lots of them, as a matter of fact. Eventually, she concluded that the house has a portal in it, a doorway to worlds from other dimensions. That would explain the ugly troll problem and tall shadow men.

As it turns out, there's this old chimney that runs up and down through the house. The rooms that have the most activity have the chimney running through it. We figured that's where the trolls are coming from. That's when I made it a point to have my Dad crank the heat up at night. Not just to stay warmer in the chilly Minnesota winters, more importantly to try to burn the trolls, or at least smoke them out. Unfortunately, it didn't help. If anything it only made them angrier.

We had the other usual annoyances in a haunted house: moving tables, moving chairs, clocks taken off the wall. The funniest incident was when my mother put a mousetrap behind the oven. Later that night she heard a commotion in the kitchen. She went in to see what was making all the noise, but found nothing. The next day she reached into one of the kitchen drawers and found the mousetrap in it, sprung. I chuckled to think about some poor troll sneaking behind the oven, only to be caught in the mousetrap!

It seems like this paranormal stuff follows me around. I moved out of my parent's house a few years back, moving to a house in Hastings. Within a few weeks, strange things began to happen there, too. Cupboard doors opening and closing on their own, and furniture moving around. As it turns out, the house was built where an old house was torn down – one that had a family murdered in. That could explain the weird things happening.

Wherever I go, I sometimes can feel strange things. Nothing like the trolls in my bedroom closet. But I still feel some strange presence. I don't like to think about the beady-red eyes, but sometimes I wake up at night, wondering if the eyes will be there, staring at me and waiting for me to scream.

HISTORY

TWIT (TUNE WHILE I TYPE)
NOT DEAD YET BY STYX

I pulled into the McDonalds in Cannon Falls and waited to interview a mother and daughter who had experienced some strange things in a house they lived in near Eastside Park. I was expecting a few annoying ghosts turning lights on and off. Perhaps even the occasional car keys or book being mysteriously misplaced. Certainly nothing monsterish. I wasn't prepared for monstrous demonic trolls.

The key element in the one hundred plus year-old house was this chimney running through it. They repeatedly made a comment about it, as if perhaps it was a portal into other worlds. Yes, portal, and other worlds. That's apparently where the trolls were coming from. Short little guys, staring at you from the slats in the door of your closet. Can't get much creepier than that. Unless they came out once and awhile and hung out at the foot of your bed. Which is what they liked to do to the daughter.

Not just the end of your bed, but they also liked to stand on the side of the bed, staring at you inches from your face while you slept, or tried to sleep. I'm thinking I'd be changing the sheets on my bed quite often in that house. Not to mention my pajamas. There's two things that really creep me out: dolls and trolls. I can handle the poltergeist activity (for the most part), and the occasional shadowy thing out of the corner of my eye. But staring point plank at a troll with beady-red eyes, or a doll grinning at me, would be just too much.

As I said, the rooms that were connected to a chimney going through the house seemed to have the most activity. That was where

the daughter and her sister stayed. Both of them have experienced the trolls. They would hear them walking around at night from one side of the bed to the other. It started at a young age; the daughter remembers seeing the troll at nine months old. Later, at five years of age, she started seeing it more frequently, and closer to her. Screaming was her best defense, for every time she screamed when she saw one, it would disappear.

The mother was not left out of the excitement. She never saw trolls, but instead saw very tall shadowy figures. She felt they were men, and were not at all too friendly. Several times she would find herself confronted with one of them, each time terrified even more than the other times. Eventually, the tall shadow figures would leave, but her memory of them never would. Even though she no longer lives in the house, she worries they will return. She even claims to have taken a picture of a shadow figure. Unfortunately, I did not have the opportunity to see it.

The house itself has had lots of other paranormal activity. Furniture at any given time can be found moved from one location in the house to another. TVs will go on and off without anyone handling the remote. Light switches do the same. And it was a common occurrence to hear footsteps running up and down the hallway late at night. Friends of the daughter during sleepovers have heard the mysterious footsteps as well.

Years ago a psychic had visited the house. She immediately knew something was wrong. After a few minutes of checking out the place, she concluded that there was a portal in it. Hence the trolls and shadow men. I'm not a big fan of portals, but I suppose they could be like worm holes, allowing you to travel from one location in the universe to another. Perhaps that's just it, these trolls aren't from another dimension, just another part of the universe.

The father has had some interesting things happen as well, including numerous scratches on his body. He would wake up to find himself scratched in various places, perplexed as to how the marks got there.

Overall, the place sounds like there are a lot of things going bump in the night. Gnarly little troll things and tall shadowy things to be exact. It definitely sounds like a place to do an investigation. Just not sure if I'd want to sleep there. Waking up to see beady-red troll eyes staring at me is not something I would look forward to. Unless perhaps it was Santa Claus with two shiny red cheeks instead. Ho-ho-ho!

House in Cannon Falls, reportedly
containing demonic trolls, shadowy
figures, and a portal into other worlds.

Artist's interpretation
of what the Hellhound
might look like.

DEMONIC HELLHOUND OF FORESTVILLE STATE PARK

"We quickly realized that we were not alone, as something in the dark distance was snapping twigs and shrubs as it moved."

I used to enjoy camping, getting out to see the great outdoors. But ever since my run in with what I call a demonic hellhound, with its glowing red eyes and tarnished pointy fangs, well, now I do all my camping at a Best Western...

I called up my best friend from high school, Jeff, to see if he wanted to do some camping on the weekend. Both of us had gone off to college and had not seen each other for over a month.

"Great! Thanks, Tom, for asking. This weekend works fine. Where should we go?" Jeff sounded eager to do some serious camping, not that we were that hardcore with it, but the few times we've gone, it had been enjoyable.

"Forestville State Park," I replied. "It's about thirty minutes east of where I grew up in Austin. They have some hiking trails and an old cave to explore."

"Sounds like fun. Would you believe I'm still packed from the last trip? Not sure how stinky the rain gear is, or the tent."

We had camped out at Nerstrand Park during the summer, which turned out to be a disaster. It had rained the entire weekend. If his stuff was still packed, it would probably be very smelly. Moldy too. "Don't worry about the packing. Just grab the essentials. I have my parent's camper this time. Should be tons of fun."

On Friday afternoon, Jeff met me at my parent's house. I was busy hitching up the camper to my Jeep when he pulled into the driveway. My parents had gone south already for the winter, even though it was only September. I wondered when the Minnesota cold would get to me, turning me into a snowbird and travel south to the warm weather each year. I got up and waved to Jeff, coming over to shake his hand. "Jeff. Great to see you again. Go ahead and throw your gear inside while I finish with the hitch."

Jeff climbed inside the camper, and a moment later I heard him yell, "Ahhh!"

The scream startled me, making my hand slip on the wheel crank for the hitch, slamming my hand into the sharp metal frame. "Ahhh!" I echoed back to Jeff from the pain, angry because of my now chewed-up knuckles with blood. Jeff came bolting out of the camper and threw something at me. I instinctively caught the thing, and then dropped it as I realize it was a dead rat. A real big one, too. And big-time stinky.

Jeff laughed. "What the heck are your parents doing with a dead rat in the fridge? And boy, does it reek in there."

"Not sure," I said, staring at the rat's lifeless whiskers and yellowed buckteeth. "Must have crawled in and died."

Jeff kicked the rat in front of me while covering his nose, "You got that right. That thing stinks."

I tossed the rat in a bag and threw it in the garbage.

With the sun dropping close to the horizon, we hopped in my Jeep and headed for the park. Most of our talk centered around our experiences with the first month of college; I had gone to Minnesota State Mankato, Jeff had gone east to University of Eau Claire, Wisconsin. Both of our experiences were similar, about the serious studying needed, the major house parties, and the fantastic looking girls everywhere you turned. But we both agreed that even with all the exciting changes in our lives, it was great to be back home for a while, and hang out with old friends.

"Hey," said Jeff, "I see the entrance to the park up ahead."

We pulled into the Ranger Station on the right to check in. The parking lot wasn't full, which meant there wouldn't be very many campers. Of course, not too many want to camp in the cold month of October. But we had the camper complete with heater, so we'd stay plenty warm.

The Park Ranger finished checking us in and gave us our permit. He looked at us and said, "No parties, right? And quiet time is 10 p.m."

Although we did bring a case of Schmidt beer, we had no plans of making this trip a drunk fest. I nodded to the Park Ranger in agreement that we would be quiet. I only wish the demonic hellhound would have obeyed the ranger's request.

The Park Ranger then added, "Oh, and one last thing. There's a bear in the forest, so be careful where you leave your food."

Jeff and I looked at each other, surprised. There had not been a bear sighted in Southeastern Minnesota for years.

The Park Ranger saw our expression of shock and added, "A family camping two weekends ago heard something foraging in the woods around midnight. Gave them quite the scare, especially when it entered their campsite and began smashing their cooler and camping chairs."

I gulped and asked, "Was anyone in the family hurt?"

Park Ranger laughed and said, "Absolutely not. Mom and Dad grabbed the kids and hopped in the car. Within seconds they were out of there." He could see we were bothered by the story and added, "Don't worry about the bear, or whatever it was. Just keep your food in your camper, or high up on a rope in a tree."

"Thanks," I said, not too sure about camping with a bear around. Of course, I knew bears were just as scared of humans as we were of them. Rattling some pans would do the trick, unless it was a grizzly bear. In worst case, they could play dead. As long as it was "play" dead, and not "real" dead.

Jeff and I pulled into the campgrounds, searching for our campsite, lucky number 13. We weren't too pleased with the number assignment, but neither of us were that superstitious. After a long winding road, we found a sign directing us further into the woods for the campsites 10 through 15. Several minutes passed before we finally arrived at the site. No other campers were at the other campsites, and since it was dark already, we doubted any others would show up.

Within only a few minutes, we had unhitched the camper and started a blazing campfire. We sat back peacefully drinking in our chairs drinking a few beers, absorbing the cool breeze and woodsy smell of the damp forest floor.

Our rest didn't last long. We quickly realized that we were not alone as something in the dark distance was snapping twigs and shrubs as it moved.

We both turned to look at where the noise was coming from. Thoughts of a wild bear leaping out of the woods made me nervous. I grabbed my whittling knife, ready for action.

Jeff laughed. "Like your knife will help save us from a bear! But I doubt there's any bears around here."

I put my knife away as the sounds of shrubs moving dissipated. "You're right. I'd be better off shoving my arm down the bear's throat."

We both laughed that at that, when suddenly something jumped out of the darkness, landing on top of our fire and sending a huge flurry of flame and ash into the air. We jumped back fast, not wanting it to burn us.

"What the heck was that?" said Jeff as he fell backward in his chair.

I looked in the fire to see what it was and couldn't believe it. "It's a rat. Another one of those dead rats."

"Whew!" said Jeff. "Yeah, now I smell it. It's worse barbequed like that. Get that thing off the fire!"

After several attempts, we were able flick the dead rat off. We threw it in a bag over to the side of our campsite. But no sooner had we sat down to enjoy another beer when more shrubs were moving and twigs snapping somewhere out in the darkness. It was apparently going to be a busy night.

This time both of us instinctively took out our whittling knifes, not at all wanting another dead rat thrown at us. I looked into the dark shadows beyond the campfire as I told Jeff, "It has to be some kids playing around with us."

Jeff said, "Yeah, I think so." He turned and yelled toward the rustling in the darkness. "Whoever you are, stop throwing the dead rats!" Then he added as he looked at his watch, "It's past quiet time, and I've also got a knife."

At that same moment, something once again flew at them, but this time it smacked Jeff right in the face, sending him falling backward. Unfortunately, the fire was also behind him. He landed right in the fire. I don't know how, but he didn't seem to get burned. Sure, his pants were smoldering a bit, and the other dead rat thrown at him was burning just fine, but Jeff wasn't.

"That was weird," I said as I helped Jeff out of the fire.

Jeff didn't say anything, too stunned with the thought of almost being barbequed.

We decided to search the area with our flashlights for whoever was causing the pranks. After twenty minutes we found no one. With the desire to sit around the campfire gone, we decided to head into the camper and play some cards. Jeff put out the fire and I went to get rid of the two dead rats. But they were both gone.

"That's odd, where'd the bag of rats go?" I asked.

"Beats me. They should be right over there. Maybe the bear took them back," said Jeff with a chuckle.

We settled into the camper, cracking open a couple more beers and setting the poker chips out to be counted. Several games of poker played on, with Jeff seeming to be the lucky one. After an hour of playing, he was up twenty bucks.

Smiling, Jeff said, "This must be my lucky day."

At that moment we heard a horrific snarling noise right outside the camper, followed by a jolt that nearly flipped it on its side.

"What the –" was all I could say before several more thumps hit the camper. Wham! Wham! Wham! There was a hideous snarling noise, as if a humongous rabid dog were standing outside our front door.

Then I saw it. I looked out the window to see two crimson eyes staring into the window. I could also see drooling sharp fangs, big ones, pointing out of this creature's long snout.

"It's the bear!" yelled Jeff, who had not looked out the window at what I saw. I knew it wasn't a bear. Then again, I didn't know what it was. But it howled like a wolf.

I turned to Jeff and said, "Does a bear howl?"

"Then what is it?"

"Don't know. And I don't want to find out."

Now the camper was rocking back and forth, with each side raising several feet off the ground. This creature was powerful. Just then, the door to the fridge opened up, and the bag of burnt rats fell out.

"How did they get in there?" asked Jeff as he tumbled back and forth.

"Beats me," I replied. For some reason I had this idea that the strange hellish dog beast outside wanted the rats. It didn't make any sense to me, but I knew what to do. "Throw them out the door," I yelled to Jeff.

Jeff looked at the door, then back at me. "I'm not opening the door. What if that thing comes in here?"

The camper was really rocking now. Several times it nearly flipped completely sideways. I held onto the bathroom door and yelled, "In a few more seconds I think that thing will be in anyway!"

That was enough for Jeff. He pulled and pushed his way over to the door with the bag of burned rats, opened the door and threw them out. As he went to close the door, the creature stuck its head into the camper. Its glowing red eyes stared at both of us for a second, and drool from its sharp fangs dropped to the steps. The creature then reached up at Jeff's wrist, slicing it open with one of its claws. "Rats!" yelled the creature in a raspy voice.

"Ahhh!" yelled Jeff as blood began to drip from his wrist.

As Jeff fell to the ground in shock, the creature turned to look at me. I looked around for a weapon to protect us with. The only thing I could find as I fell back into the bathroom was a toilet scrubby brush. Now I can tell you one thing, I'm not at all ashamed to have beaten down this Hellhound thing with a toilet scrubby, but I did. I think the chemicals (or other smells) scared the thing off. As soon as I swatted the thing on the nose with the nylon bristles, it turned and fled. It grabbed the bag of dead rats, too. I never found out anything more about the rats either; I was just glad to get rid of them.

I looked at Jeff's wrist. It wasn't cut too deep, but it was bleeding enough to make a mess out of the carpet in the camper. "We need to get you to the hospital," I said.

"Sounds good to me," said Jeff. "Anything to get away from this place."

I helped Jeff into the Jeep and I went back to hitch up the camper. Or at least that was what I planned. But the Hellhound came back. I don't know, but I think he was mad about the toilet scrubby. I wasn't going to wait around to tell it I was sorry. I dropped my tools near the hitch as the creature came running at me. Thankfully, I had the door open on the Jeep so I jumped in.

I trembled with the keys, dropping them several times to the floor. When I finally got the key in the ignition, I looked and saw two things. First was Jeff, who had turned white and I think was in severe shock. Secondly, I saw why he was in shock. The Hellhound creature was standing in front of the car. It must have been eight feet tall, all hunched over and hairy from head to toe.

I slammed the key further into the ignition and started the car. The noise startled the Hellhound for a moment, but then it jumped. At first we didn't know where it went; it was as if it jumped straight up into the air. But we weren't about to get out and look for it. I shifted my Jeep into drive and tore out of the camp-site. We had made it all the way to the park before realizing where the Hellhound ended up. It was on top of the Jeep.

The creature looked down at me from the windshield. Instinctively, I slammed on the breaks. This sent the Hellhound creature flying out in front of the Jeep. As I saw it tumble several times, I panicked and began driving again, running over the creature with a thump-thump.

I ended up taking Jeff straight to the hospital in Austin where he received eight stitches to his wrist. We didn't bother trying to explain how he got the cut – nobody would believe us. But as the years fly by, I find myself thinking more about the Hellhound, how lucky we were to escape. I was glad we got away, and didn't want that thing terrorizing anyone else. So maybe telling a few people wouldn't hurt.

Just to let you know, Jeff and I never went camping again. And my parents were not at all happy with the camper. It was bashed in pretty good, and Jeff's blood was impossible to get out of the carpet. Of course the smell was the worst. That dead rat smell never went away, no matter how many times we cleaned it.

HISTORY

TWIT (TUNE WHILE I TYPE)
BARK AT THE MOON BY OZZY OSBOURNE

The source of this story came from two young men who claim to have been terrorized by some strange monster one night while camping in Southeast Minnesota. As the story goes, the two of them were camping somewhere about fifteen miles from the Iowa border. That could mean the incident happened in a number of places. But based on looking at the map, the most likely candidate would be Forestville State Park.

The park itself is pretty secluded, along with the campsites. Although I would think that for this to occur, there would be many eyewitnesses, or at least someone else hearing the sounds of the camper being beaten up. The likelihood of having some evil possessed monster dog living in the park is unlikely. Southeastern Minnesota in general is not that desolate; it's not as if you can drive for a hundred miles and still not see signs of civilization. Sure, I'll admit you could get lost in Forestville State Park, but not for long. It's not more than a several hour hike from one side to the other, although if you were disoriented, you could circle around for quite some time. But having a wild hellhound on the loose is just not probable in my opinion. Furthermore, you would have most likely had other incidents show up, of which I found none.

If something attacked the campers, I would have to agree that what they found was most likely a large bear. But even that is highly unlikely, as there hasn't been a bear found in Southeastern Minnesota in many years. Of course, this story could have been from decades ago, too.

The other thought, is that this report of a demonic hellhound could be some type of werewolf. There have been numerous reports of werewolf sightings in Wisconsin, around the Bray Road area southwest of Milwaukee. After doing my research, I could not come up with any detailed sightings in Minnesota. Could the hellhound in this story be one of them? Perhaps.

It's more likely that the hellhound could be a mutant canine. There are numerous reports of mutant canines across Minnesota. Larger than your average dog, these animals are more wolf-like than anything. In fact, that could very well be what they are. Minnesota is home to wolves, wild dogs, and plenty of coyotes. One individual, while traveling home to Le Sueur on Highway 169 along the Minnesota River, thought he literally saw the big bad wolf. The creature walked out of the woods nearby, with the man initially thinking it was a small deer, but it was much larger than that. And bigger than a coyote as well.

A mutant canine was also reported about twenty minutes north of the Twin Cities, in a local park. The man was out late at night, walking his two small dogs, when a large animal, similar to a canine, came within twenty to thirty feet of them. It was light cream in color, with long fur on the underbelly, and shorter hair on top. The eyes were dark brown, and the face reminded him of a husky, but the rest of the body was more like a wolf, with short, pointy ears. It turned and looked at the man briefly, snarling a moment, before turning and running back into the woods.

Whether it's some demonic hellhound, a wandering werewolf, or a mutant canine, there's obviously something out there in Minnesota late at night. And let's not forget the coyotes or wolves that live here. Perhaps there's a crossbreed between them and dogs? Possibly. All I know is I keep a closer watch on my dogs (and myself) when I walk them late at night.

Fieldtrip

I've camped many times in Southeastern Minnesota, and although it can get somewhat spooky out late at night, I've never heard of any strange creatures attacking campers. Although just recently there was an attack up north, in Itasca State Park, weeks before we were headed up for a Boy Scout campout. Needless to say, there were several stories on that trip about spooky animals lurking near your tent while you slept.

Stopping in at Forestville State Park is like any other Minnesota State Park, at least for the parks in Central and Southern Minnesota. It has a quiet camping area for your tent or camper, and has some great woods for hiking. With my digital recorder running, I walked through the area, trying to see if there were any restless spirits lingering. I found myself enjoying the walk around; it was very peaceful and relaxing. No bears or hellhounds to be found. Later investigation of the digital records did not reveal any EVPs (Electronic Voice Phenomena – voices left by spirit beings on recorders).

This illustration
depicts a possible hybrid
creature, somewhere between
a dog and a wolf, which could
be similar to some of the beasts
sighted around Minnesota.

One of several paths within Forestville State Park, where the Hellhound supposedly resides.

I'm working with a Boy Scout Troop that's thinking of going camping at Forestville State Park perhaps next year. I'm not sure if I'll mention the story about this Hellhound, though. They may not want to go then. Or perhaps it would be exciting, making them want to camp there even more. You never know. But I know for sure it would make a great story to tell around the flickering campfire. I just hope it doesn't come true while we're there.

The other location I traveled to, even if it isn't in Minnesota, was Bray Road just southwest of Milwaukee, Wisconsin. I couldn't resist. After all, how many chances do you get to check out a famous location where werewolves live? The only trouble was convincing my son to go along with it. We had just been in Milwaukee, competing at a Jr. U.S. Open Chess Tournament (which his school came in first place), and decided to take a road trip through werewolf country.

He didn't mind of course, being he had his Nintendo DS with him. It was getting a bit late in the day, but I could still see the country side as we pulled up to Bray Road. It's mostly farm fields, with the occasional plot of land where a farm house and barn was situated. We drove around the area for awhile, keeping close to Bray Road, and looking intently for any signs of werewolves. Of course, I wasn't sure what that would be, other than some six-foot-tall hairy creatures, or massively large paw prints in the mud.

But we found none of this at the time. Perhaps we'll take a trip back there again sometime, but late at night during the witching hour. Then maybe we'll find a werewolf or two. Of course, I'm not sure what I'd do at that point, other than run like crazy in the opposite direction. But not before asking nicely to take its picture.

ELF OF LAKE HARRIET

"The monster was the best friend I ever had."

– Boris Karloff
(English horror movie actor, 1887-1969)

I, am an elf, who lives in a tree.

No, I am not a tall, slender elf as seen in the movies or books by Tolkien (Yes, I've read them!). I'm more of the type found in Ireland, or Iceland. The "Little Folk," as some would call us. Like a Leprechaun, but even smaller. I resent being called little, as I believe my heart stands to be larger than a dinosaur, and twice as strong.

Many call me Mr. Little Guy, but my real name is Thom. I've lived in the Minneapolis area from before it was, well, Minneapolis. Back in the lumberjack days, when it was a major trade route of timber via the grand Mississippi River. The name Minneapolis was coined from a schoolmaster I befriended back in the 1800s. We heard the Dakota Native Americans (from the Mdewakanton tribe) talk about all the water around here; they used the word *Mni*, or at least that's how it was pronounced. And city in Greek is *polis*. So *Mnipolis* made sense to us. Too bad they ended up spelling it wrong. Oh well. It was no concern of mine. The life of an elf transcends such worries. Or so I thought.

I came to America back in the early 1800s, from Ireland. Sure, I spent a hundred years or so in Iceland, but I found that too cold for my taste (although Minnesota isn't much better!). I wanted to get away from things, in particular, my relatives. Don't get me wrong, I love my heritage and culture. But sometimes I needed some space. America, in the early 1800s, was vast. Plenty of room to get lost in.

But then the Europeans came. They not only frustrated and destroyed the Native American way of life, but they also totally ruined my plans of seclusion. I had a great agreement with the Dakota tribes; they don't bother me, and I won't turn them into toads and curse their families for generations. The Europeans, however, didn't really believe in me. It's hard to work your mojo if a person doesn't believe you exist.

Over the decades, I was forced to limit my excursions. No more travels to Duluth, Bemidji, Mankato, or Rochester. I have friends in all of these places. No, it was too risky to make the journey. It's not like I had to go places to visit; my magic let me go anywhere I wanted. But it takes a lot of power to use magic, which drains you physically, mentally, and spiritually.

Photo of the proposed elf, Mr. Little Guy,
who lives in a tree off Lake Harriet.

Nowadays, I spend my time at the lake—Lake Harriet. It's very peaceful here, except for the numerous seagulls (a.k.a. lakegulls), on the beach looking for a snack. I end up with a decent meal now and then, when a bird decides to mess with me. One, "Zap!" of my magic, and "Poof!," the bird's done better than a Peking roasted duck at LeeAnn Chins.

One thing I'd like to mention, is how the world is changing. All this technology is, well, replacing the old way of magic. Many of my Elvin friends say that technology is the new magic. I suppose they're right, to some extent. But I don't like it. What's wrong with keeping the old way? Creating things out of nothing, instantly traveling from place to place, transforming into different things. It's all still fun to me, that is if I could do it.

You see, the magic is disappearing, and me along with it. Magic comes from belief; the more you believe, the more you have magic. It's quite simple really. But everything's science and technology, so the belief in the unknown is drying up. The power in the Great Ether, floating around us, is all but gone. I can barely tie my shoes someday. And traveling to other lands, or worlds, well, that's just not possible. Way too much work.

I'm worried that my time on this planet is limited. I'd never thought that before, Elves live forever, right? Well, I'm beginning to think a person only lives as long as the Belief lives. Belief, with a capital "B," stands for everything you believe in. And when that dies, you die with it. Right now, I'm hanging on by the slender strand of a silkworm's thread.

Thankfully, I have found a few who still believe.

The children of Minneapolis still believe. A few of them at least. And perhaps in me writing this letter, more will join together and see my truth. Which truth is that you ask? The truth in believing the unknown and impossible: to dance between the stars twinkling at night, to soar with eagles from mountain top to mountain top, and to swim alongside the dolphins from the Pacific to the Atlantic – all in one night.

Let me ask you something. When you walk by a tree, what do you see? Hmm? If your answer is, "just a tree," well, then, you do not believe. Look again at a tree, the next time you are walking through the woods. Look very closely at its base. Do you see something then? A door perhaps? That door you see, is the entrance to an Elf House. That door, is the entrance to the unknown and impossible.

Will you open it? Do you believe? Seeing is believing, but that is only part of it. Doing is needed. Open the door, come on in, and visit with your local Elf. We are everywhere, by the way. You just can't see us. Unless you believe, of course.

I have many who open my door, at the base of a tree on the south side of Lake Harriet. Everyone is welcome, but few come in. Mostly it's children, asking questions, hoping for something better, wondering about the unknown and questioning the impossible. The children of Minneapolis write letters to me, putting them inside my door, hoping and waiting for my response. I do not disappoint them. Every letter is read and answered. Yet, my magic is not absolute; sometimes the response never gets all the way back to the sender. That, sadly, breaks my heart.

I have, however, contacted the United States Postal Service for help. They have given me a P.O. Box to use, when my magic is weak and I can't respond as quickly as I'd like, or for when I'm visiting family and friends in my homeland, back in Ireland from time to time. But even there, the magic is weakening. None of us visit much anymore; perhaps once a year at best. Sometimes it's difficult to carry on.

But I must continue. There is always hope, right? Hope for a better day, a better world, like it was before. And my hope comes from your letters. You see, the letters are my strength, they are my door into this world. They help me remain. And for that, I thank all the children of Minneapolis and its surrounding area.

So the next time you walk past a tree, in the woods or park or backyard, look closer and see if there's a door. If so, open it and visit for awhile. Send me a letter. I promise I will read it. And I will sign it, like I always do, with, "I believe in you." The real question is, *do you believe in me?*

HISTORY

TWIT (TUNE WHILE I TYPE)

IN DARKEST DREAMS BY THE TANGENT

I know what you're thinking. Why on earth would I put a happy, jolly, rosy-cheeked tree elf in a monster book? Well, honestly, I thought perhaps a change was needed. After all, who wants to read about scary, life-threatening monsters wreaking death and destruction in the whole book? Er, well, of course I do—and probably yourself, since you bought this book (or picked it up in the library). Still, let us remember that a monster is not always what it seems (remember Frankenstein).

With the story above, however, it's exactly what it is. An elf, living in a tree, downtown Minneapolis, spreading happiness, warmth, and joy. What else is there? Apparently in Minnesota, there are no other types of elves—none that I could find anyway. Although there is one story I found that was intriguing.

A young man from a small northern Minnesota town, of Irish decent, claims to have had a dangerous run in with an elf. The town area was settled mainly by Scandinavians, which in their mythology, the elves are sometimes called Huldefolk (which translates basically to Hidden Folk). Boys would sometimes go to the caves outside of town, to throw rocks in them and taunt the Hidden Folk. Some teenagers would actually get up enough nerve to go into the caves, but the caves smelled awful, like something had been dead in them for months.

Every once in awhile, the Hidden Folk would be spotted, usually at dusk, presumably when they were out beginning their search for food. And many times, farmers would wake up in the morning with several hens gone, including their eggs. It was assumed by many, that the stories were made up, to prevent others from running around late

at night and stealing poultry, vegetables, or apples from the orchards. For the most part, it worked, with many Scandinavians as well as the Irish in town fearful of the elves coming out at night.

One day, in the early evening of summer, the young man was walking down a deer path when farther up the trail he could see a small, stocky man, with spiky black hair, sunken dark eyes, and a huge nose. He smiled to show uneven yellowing teeth. The stocky man was definitely a stranger (being that you typically knew everyone because the town was so small), dressed in a bib overall and filthy cotton shirt, and had no shoes on, showing his enormous feet which were covered in dense, black hairs.

The stranger kept staring at the young man's new boots and blue jeans, and obviously wanted them. Within seconds, the stocky stranger wrestled the young man to the ground bent on taking his boots and pants. Fortunately, the young man was a wrestler, so under normal conditions could easily handle the stocky man. But the stocky man began to grow, to at least twice his size. That was the young man's queue to turn and run. He only looked back twice, both times seeing the now tall, hulking man pounding his way along the trail, close behind. Eventually, the young man made it home, with the stranger no longer following.

I have to admit, it's not one of the most exciting stories, but it's from Minnesota at least. So in theory, there are elves in the area. Going about proving that, is another thing altogether. Especially if they have special magical powers, or can appear and disappear in an instant. Perhaps that's why there's no stories about them; they are much more clever at not getting caught than your average Bigfoot, Wendigo, or lake monster (after all, the elves are called Hidden Folk for a reason).

But just to make things interesting, I thought I'd pass along a couple stories about elves from other parts of the world. Apparently, they are much more prevalent elsewhere. Take the case of workers in a herring-processing plant in Iceland, back in 1962. Supposedly in Iceland, landowners always leave a bit of green space when constructing buildings, to provide room for the elves living underground. But the owners of the herring plant chose not to. And, as they began building the foundation, drill bits would mysterious shatter. It wasn't until an Elf Seer came and convinced the elves to move that the

The Elf of Lake Harriet's proposed home, in a tree
just down from South Oliver Avenue.

construction of the new building went flawlessly. Of course, I was very much interested in finding out what the Elf Seer said to the elves.

In another case, there was the report of an elf, or some type of entity, protecting a cabin out in the northeast part of the U.S. Two kids were happily swimming outside on the beach, but not before they had previously started a fire in their cabin, in the fireplace. When they returned to the cabin, they found the fire had gotten out of control, with the nearby curtains on fire. While they stood there and screamed (as their parents were not around at the time), they watched as something was moving around the room, frantically trying to beat out the flames. Within minutes, the fire was subdued, with only a smoke-filled room and char-coaled curtains and rug. They have had many occurrences in the cabin like that, all of which they attribute to an elf taking care of the place.

So while there apparently isn't much activity in Minnesota, there is out in the rest of the world. And not just your cute little leprechaun looking dudes. Many times, elves are just considered intelligent energy (which could also include angels, fairies, dwarves, etc.). Basically there's a certain level of natural energy, channeled into a particular being, or shape-shifting into whatever it wants to be. This, of course, gets into the realm of being virtually impossible to prove. If the elves are that far advanced to us, well, there's not much we can do about it. I very much doubt they're going to slow down enough to let us take their picture on purpose. And even if they did, they might use their hocus-pocus and remove the image from the camera. Who knows? It's magic, right?

So in a nutshell, yes, there are supposedly magical elves living in Minnesota. Some more visible (a.k.a Lake Harriet Elf), some much more stealthy. But perhaps this is a great opportunity to try and find more of them? Is there any new technology which may capture their presence? Or, being that they are allegedly highly intelligent, maybe they're open to reason. Instead of fancy gizmos, we just ask nicely? Show yourself Mr. Elf! I promise I won't offend you with my lowly human brainpower. Just don't turn me into a newt when I start asking dumb questions.

FIELDTRIP

I decided it would be fun to try and find this famous Lake Harriet Elf, or at least get a glimpse of his humble abode, a.k.a. tree. From various sources, I determined it to be located along the walking paths around Lake Harriet, near South Oliver Avenue.

Of course, I was hoping to visit with the elf, chat for a few minutes in the warm confines of his tree. Sadly, I arrived too late; Mr. Little Guy had gone south for the winter already. But he did leave a P. O. Box number on his door. There were also a few notes wrapped in plastic near his door, most likely from a few souls late in the season, curious about the lives of elves, and why he chooses to live in a tree.

The wooden door to his home in the tree is there, but locked up until spring. I have not sent him a note, but perhaps I should. I need to find out a few things. At the top of the list would be to verify if he's real. Of course, any answer will do. Regardless of who is behind all this elf mischief, the goodness that unfolds from this is worth a thousand magical moments. Magic, in many cases, is done with ordinary means, but through extraordinary circumstances.

So my conclusion is that in a magical way, the elf, Mr. Little Guy, living off Lake Harriet, down from South Oliver Avenue, is real. Real enough to change the hearts of those who can see the door in the tree, which can open their heart to a magical world of faith, hope, and love.

Grizzly bear like the ones that used to
inhabit Minnesota over a century ago.
This one looks a bit angry.

GIANT BOUNDARY WATERS BEAR

"Never moon a Werewolf."

– Anonymous

I'd like to think I'm an expert camper, always cautious of my surroundings, always ready for anything. But when a giant bear wakes you in the dead of night, well, there's not much for you to do, but scream bloody murder.

Camping in the Boundary Waters Canoe Area, BWCA as it's called, can be one of the most rewarding experiences in life. Getting back to nature, in a location with no electricity, no cars, and no motors, should be tried by all. But take heed; it is not for the faint of heart. Not with all the mosquitoes, elk, timber wolves, and bears. And did I mention there's no McDonalds?

Yes, food must either be carried in (and the remains carried out, commonly known as the Yum-Yum Bag, full of uneaten, smelly food), or found. By "found" I mean hunted, which I was no good at. Sure, I do the occasional fishing trip now and then, but that's about it. Most of my hunting is done at the grocery store, searching for the best price on the things I need the least of. Needless to say, all the food for my Boundary Waters trip was captured in the wild isles of Walmart and treacherous terrain of Target.

Like I said, I've camped before, many times at many state parks. My favorite is Itasca; getting to see the beginning of the Mississippi River at Lake Itasca is amazing, not to mention you have the opportunity to walk across it. But the Boundary Waters, well, this is different. Did I mention there's no bathrooms?

I convinced a buddy of mine, Bruce, to go camping with me. He doesn't do any outdoor stuff, which should have probably been my first clue not to invite him. Still, you really need someone else to go with, in case of emergencies. Going solo into such a wild place is asking for trouble; like trying to play the Timberwolves—the basketball team that is, when you're only four-foot-nine. Of course, the real timber wolves—the kinds found in the forests of northern Minnesota—would most likely give you a similar disastrous result.

"Are you going to eat *all* the Doritos?" I asked Bruce, as we paddled around a bend in the southwest side of Fall Lake, on our way up to Pipestone Bay. Actually, *I* was the one paddling; Bruce was busy eating our only bag of chips.

Bruce shook his head while wiping his cheesy hands on his jeans. "Tom, Tom, Tom. Do you think I'm that selfish?" He reached into the bag for more, only to realize it was empty. He looked up at me with cheesy lips and said, "Oops."

I paused, wondering if I should answer honestly. Starting a fight in the middle of nowhere is never a good idea. I had to rely on Bruce, and he on me. It was best not to create a feud on the first day of our excursion. I had a feeling, however, the grudge work was inevitable, most likely ensuing by the last day, or sooner.

Opting to continue the use of my paddle in the water, and not on Bruce's head, I answered, "Of course you're not selfish." I stared at the empty bag of Doritos, licking my lips. My stomach churned, sending a loud rippling echo across the lake to the trees beyond.

"Chill out, man," said Bruce while rummaging through his backpack. "I brought an extra bag of munchies." He tossed the empty bag overboard (which I promptly retrieved), then ripped open a new one. "Always be prepared!"

"You're a junk food junkie," I said while continuing to paddle, eyebrows lowered. I purposefully slapped the water, sending a splash of cold lake water at Bruce, careful as not to get the Doritos wet.

Bruce quickly covered the bag with his arms, protecting his tasteful and lone source of civilization. "You nuts?" He hugged the bag gently as not to crush the tender and flavorful contents. "This is my only foundation of happiness." Then he scowled at me and added, "I'm not sure why I agreed to go on this wild trip." He munched quietly on the fresh chips, staring past the lake and trees, far into the wilderness. I suppose he was keeping an eye out for something more familiar, like a road, or a Wendy's, or maybe a Best Buy. As for myself, I was watching out for bears.

I read up on the furry creatures; they shouldn't be a problem, unless you're stupid. I was pretty sure of myself not doing something dumb to attract a bear. But Bruce? That was a different story. One that probably ended with black fur, sharp claws, an angry growl, and a dash of pepper spray.

I couldn't have been closer to the truth.

Having paddled for what seemed like forever and a day, we finally reached Pipestone Bay. I have to say, for as much work as it was getting there, it was worth it. They say the Boundary Waters is God's Country, still pristine and golden, like the old days. I would agree wholeheartedly. But even the Garden of Eden had the Snake. Here, well, there were mosquitoes.

"Where'd they all come from?" asked Bruce while continuously swatting, more at the air than anything else. He began spraying the air around him with Off, while I was busy setting up the tent.

"You're supposed to wear the insect repellant, not breath it."

A moment later, Bruce ran off toward the canoe, still spraying, and now yelling, "Die! Die! Die!" to the infestation of mosquitoes following him. He was like some World War II movie hero, launching himself recklessly from a trench into the front line of fight. I would have much rather preferred Bruce staying and helping me with the tent. Maybe. It was getting dark, the time at which the mosquitoes were in full swing. Once the sun set, however, all would be better. I hoped. But until then, we needed protection from the stinging, blood-sucking, vampire creatures. The best way was to sit in your tent and wait it out.

Darkness came, the mosquitoes went, and Bruce puked in our tent.

"Too much junk food?" I smirked as Bruce ran outside (after several attempts to push himself through the zipped door.

"I think I swallowed a billion bugs," he gagged. "Don't... feel... so good."

"Yeah, and the tent don't smell so good either." I began cleaning up the mess. *What am I, his mother?* "You probably inhaled too much bug spray."

I should have let Bruce sleep out in the canoe. But the thought of having to tend to his mosquito bites all morning didn't sound too appealing. By then he'd be more bite than body. Probably would have turned into a mosquito for all I knew. No, the best place for Bruce was out of harm's way, in the puke-smelling tent.

"Feeling better?" I asked, trying to sound as sincere as possible.

"Uh-huh," replied Bruce, his teeth chattering from the confines of his sleeping bag. I won't go into much detail, but being that October was fast approaching in the Great Northern Woods of Minnesota, the temperature at night was dipping close to freezing. Bruce's thin, fleece sleeping bag wouldn't cut it. Lord knows I'm willing to help out my fellow man. But I wasn't about to share my sleeping bag with him. No way.

Thankfully, Bruce was still wearing his clothes from the day, plus some. He would not freeze, I kept saying to myself. Although that would make the trip back a lot quieter and less stressful. People would ask, "How was your BWCA trip?" and I'd reply, "Good. My stupid friend froze to death." But then there'd be no one to help back up my story about the growling and shuffling outside the tent. *Growling? Shuffling?*

"You hear that?" I asked while perking my head up from the comfort of my travel pillow.

Bruce was eating Doritos again. Third bag of apparently only one. "Sorry, what?" The spicy aroma of chips was wafting from his fleece bag.

"You're eating? In the tent?" I whispered.

"What?" Munch, munch, munch... "I was hungry."

"What part of, put-all-food-in-the-food-sack-and-hang-it-from-the-tree don't you understand?"

Bruce stopped eating for a moment and asked, "Hey, you hear something?"

"Duh," I said, now wondering if I should throw him out the front of the tent, like a sacrificial lamb to the mysterious creature lurking outside.

"What is it?" asked Bruce, sitting up and peering at the shadows on the tent that the creature was making. "It looks huge."

I was pretty sure what it was, but I didn't want to alarm Bruce. There's no telling what he'd do. Actually, I knew exactly what he'd do. He'd scream like a little girlie-boy, then run out of the tent.

And that's what he did.

The yelling part was a good thing; that's what you do with black bears. Brown bears, too. But running? Nope. Bad idea. A bear will outrun you every time. Unless it has other, more important things to do. Like feed on a half-eaten bag of Doritos.

Yes, it's true. Doritos saved Bruce's life. Mine, too, I suppose. While Bruce ran for the shelter of the canoe, he had tossed the bag of chips. Of course, it wasn't actually that simple. When Bruce popped out of the tent, the bear, in its growling fury, was there, hungry no doubt. It was huge, over ten feet tall, standing, its yellow teeth as big as my fingers, and its glossy eyes larger than billiard balls. And when it growled, the earth shook, vibrating my already quivering knees.

But as I said, the bear was mesmerized by the artificially flavored cheesy chips (aren't we all?). I briefly wondered if corn chips would have done the job, or maybe pretzels. If I were a bear, it would have to be something layered with cheese. Nachos perhaps. Or maybe lasagna. But I digress.

Large brown bear rummaging through the grass looking for food, which hopefully doesn't include you, unless you smell like Doritos.

There was only one thing to do. Well, two things. One, of course, had to do with soiling my underwear (a third was screaming like a little girl—which I had already done several times over). The other was running for the canoe. I wasn't worried though. I had pepper spray. Yeah, right. Could I actually trust my life with a tiny vial of liquid peppers? What if it only annoyed the bear? I guess there's not much difference between an annoyed bear and a hungry one. Both will still eat you.

With pepper spray in hand, like a Colt 45 (no not the beer kind), I slowly stepped out of the tent and shuffled toward the canoe. And as I suspected, about the time I was halfway to the canoe (and only a few yards from Mr. Bear), the Doritos bag of everlasting goodness ran dry.

The giant bear was not happy.

It turned to face me with its wild, cheesy snout shifting back and forth in the air, trying to smell if I had chips as well, or maybe if I was made of cheese. Either way, I was probably his next meal.

There is one brilliant moment in Bruce's life; I'm sure of it. And this is it: He had gathered enough brain cells together and righted the canoe in the water. I was happy with that and began to run toward it. Sadly, I wasn't part of his plan. I knew this because he was quickly paddling out from shore—without me.

"Wait!" I yelled, while spraying pepper wildly behind me. Would the pepper only add to the flavor of the chips? A *Late at Night Jalapeño Doritos Snack* perhaps?

I splashed into the water, my arms flapping in panicked windmill fashion, not looking back. There was no point in watching the bear pounce on me. I had to use every ounce of energy I had to swim to the canoe. Thankfully, Bruce had slowed down. Or maybe it was that he couldn't figure out how to paddle.

"Relax!" said Bruce as he reached to pull me in, nearly flipping the canoe. "The bear's gone."

I paused a moment, listening. Far into the distance I could hear the howling of a hurt bear.

"What did you spray him with, acid?"

I heaved myself into the canoe, flopping down in the bottom, sucking in huge volumes of air. "Something like that."

Since then I've camped many times at BWCA. None with Bruce. Or Doritos. And I can't say for sure if it was a giant bear or not. All I know is that it was big enough to kill me. A monster isn't always measured by its size; but by its attitude. And when cheesy snacks are involved, in the wilderness, who knows what kind of monster will arise.

HISTORY

TWIT (TUNE WHILE I TYPE)

PSYCHO KILLER BY TALKING HEADS

Let's face it. Bears are real. And to depict them as a monster is not correct. But the reality is that in some cases, bears can go a little stir-crazy. And that, my friends, is when they turn into monsters.

Don't get me wrong, I'm not blaming it on the bears. Most bear attacks are due to human error. That late night Snickers in your tent, or half-eaten bag of Doritos, or not changing your clothes before sleeping in your tent, after eating a bowl of spaghetti. The bear, with its keen nose, can sense that candy bar a mile away, or that spaghetti sauce drenched shirt probably several miles away. And can you blame him? I'm mean, come on. We're talking Snickers and Doritos here!

Needless to say, the bear will think you are the Snickers, or you are the bag of Doritos. And in the process of trying to eat your shirt filled with spaghetti, well, he might end up eating you. Not good. But again, it's not the bear's fault. You could have waited for the Snickers bar until breakfast. Or washed up before bedtime (but not with perfumy soap – that will smell just as good to a bear).

But what types of bears are we talking about. Which ones inhabit Minnesota, and where? Back before Minnesota was a state, there were several kinds of bears roaming the forest and grasslands. I'm sure everyone has heard about black bears and brown bears. But what about the ferocious grizzlies? Yes, they too once lived here. But none have been reported for decades, having been hunted out of the area nearly a century ago.

The American Black Bear (or Ursus Americanus for you scientistic folkies), however, is still very much around. While not as big and ferocious, it can still kill you in a heartbeat. They are typically four to seven feet long, nose to tail (and there's not much tail on a bear). They have small eyes, yet a big appetite, and round, furry ears on top. Oh, and did I mention the claws?

And how many are there? It's estimated that there are 750,000 of them in North America. A few are in Florida and northern Mexico, while the majority live more in the northern region of the United States. They can weigh up to 500 pounds, with a record size found in northeastern Minnesota back in 1994, a male weighing in at 876 pounds.

What's most alarming to me, is how great their senses are. While their vision is good, their hearing is evening better – much better than ours. And as far as smelling, well, it's off the charts, being a 100 times more powerful than us humans. And if that wasn't enough, their brains are large when compared to their body size. So let's just say they're not your average cow standing out in the field.

Let's not forget that they are good swimmers as well. So don't think you can hop in the lake for a quick getaway, or think you're safe camping on an island.

And as far as running goes, a bear can travel at speeds of 30 mph—uphill, downhill, you name it.

Thankfully, their preferred food is nuts, acorns, fruit, insects, and succulent greens. That is, of course, assuming you don't have any succulent Cheetos around. Still, meat is on their menu, which then includes us as a meal.

So what is the ideal habitat for a bear? Black bears like to be in forests, especially ones with fruit or nuts (i.e. oak or walnut trees). And if there's some lowlands around, it provides for tender and juicy vegetation, not to mention a great place to get a drink. They also need a large area to range. An adult male can roam from eight to fifteen miles.

All in all, it's safe to say that anywhere you go camping, hiking, or biking, and there's lots of forest around, there may be bears. Which means you may be in danger of being their next meal. And now for the most important fact: How often do bears kill people? Well, between 1900 and 2003, there were about 105 recorded deaths due to bears—52 from black bears, 50 from brown bears (or grizzlies), and 3 from polar bears.

Keep in mind, this covers over 100 years. 100 deaths (as gruesome as they were, after reading about some of them), are rare indeed. Care to guess how many campers, hikers, and bikers there are in the forests and parks around the nation? Millions of them each year (8.5 million in Yosemite National Park alone in the previous year). So technically speaking, your chances of getting killed and eaten by a bear are over a million to 1. That is, of course, if you take precautionary measures. Bringing food into your tent, or wearing filthy clothes will increase your odds of getting mauled greatly.

But the killings do happen. Take for example a man from Ely, Minnesota, back in 2007, who wandered into the woods to urinate. He never came back. He had startled a black bear, and got mauled to death. The bear was found later and killed.

Thankfully, there are not that many reports of people being killed by bears in Minnesota. Most of the incidents occur further west, in the Glacier National Park area. But that doesn't mean there won't be anyone killed in Minnesota in the future. And keep in mind, there are thousands of bear sightings, but few attacks. Perhaps this is because most people camping in Minnesota take appropriate action, to not entice the bear (i.e., no chips in the tent!). It's most important to recognize that when we go camping in places such as the Boundary Waters, we are invading the bear's territory—we are the guests. And, if done right, we will not become the meal.

Lastly, I wanted to share two of my favorite bear jokes…

So how do you know if you have black bears around, versus grizzlies? Well, with black bears, they run away if you hit them with pepper spray, or if you wear loud, clanging bells. But if you see bear scat that smells like peppers and has bells in it, then you have grizzlies.

And…

A bear walks into a local bar in Ely, pounding on the counter and growls, "I want a large rum and .... a coke."

Roger, the bartender, stops wiping the counter, looks at the bear and asks, "What's with the huge pause?"

The bear looks at his paws and answers, "Oh, them, I've had them all my life."

An angry black bear, like others roaming around northern Minnesota when we disturb them.

GIANTS OF BEMIDJI

"You can't create a monster, then whine when it stomps on a few buildings"

– Lisa Simpson
(character from The Simpsons)

I don't know why I'm called a giant. Sure, at just under ten feet tall, I'm larger than most people. I have to tell you, though, I'm no monster. At least not anymore. But that doesn't stop campers and hikers in the remote parts of northern Minnesota from screaming and running wildly away when they see me.

The name's Bonjean, Paul Bonjean. Most know me by the name Paul Bunyan. While many consider me just a myth, or legend, I assure you I'm real. Very real. And I can be your best friend, or your worst nightmare. It just depends on what you're doing up in the northern woods of Minnesota.

Originally born in Bemidji back in the mid 1800s (although it wasn't a town back then), I grew up fast, or tall I should say. By the age of ten, I was well over seven feet tall. Teased by the local Leech Lake Indians (who were the only ones there besides my family), I ran away to the big city of St. Paul, which back then had a place called Pigs Eye Landing.

I loved the night life. With my tallness, I was easily able to get into the saloons, to drink, smoke, and play poker. And with my strength, I would work during the day at Pigs Eye Landing, or Reads Landing, helping steamboats dock.

During that time, I never stopped thinking about the northern woods. The logs moving down the Mississippi River always reminded me of my heritage. I was of the trees, not brick and mortar. But what life would there be for me, a tall lumbering giant, up north in the middle of nowhere?

Frustrated, I gave up my high life in the city and joined the railroad company. I spent several years building the Great Northern Railway, and Northern Pacific Railway, doing the work of five men, sometimes ten, and getting paid just as much.

With a suitcase full of money, I decided to head back to my home in Bemidji. By now, in the late 1800s, the town was becoming a reality.

GIANT SUTTUNG AND THE DWARFS.

And sawmills were opening up off the Mississippi, sending thousands of fresh-cut white pine timber to them. That's where I began my career as a lumberjack.

The added benefit of being a lumberjack was in getting away from the public eye. Now in my 40s, I was nearly nine feet tall; a freak to most people. That angered me, and with my strength, there's no telling what I might do if pushed over the edge. No, the best thing to do was go farther into the forest.

I can't say how far I traveled, cutting timber left and right like they were bean stalks, but I'm sure it was well into Canada. The other lumberjacks couldn't keep up with me. With my strength continuing to increase (as well as my height), I was cutting and hauling an acre a day of wood to the nearby river. It wasn't until years later that I realized my mistake.

The forest I knew and loved was vanishing.

Settlers and lumberjacks were clearing it away. Worst of all, *I was one of them*. What had I done? What could I do to fix it?

By the early 1900s, I was getting old, but not showing it in the least. It seemed as though I would live forever. Yet, with every tree I felled, my heart grew weaker. It was then I realized the trees were my strength; I was here to protect them, not destroy them.

Angry with what I had done, I ran into the forest, planning never to return. Unfortunately, there wasn't much forest left. And it was easy for campers or hikers to find me. I'd scream at them to go away, throwing trees like they were toothpicks (which hurt me even more). I began to wonder if in fact I was a monster, a freak of nature not worthy of living. Yet, on my deathbed of barren ground among stumps of pine (and having not eaten for months), I found a friend just like me. His name was Babe.

Nowadays, he's thought of as Babe the Blue Ox. He's actually gray, but in the right light his thick coat of fur gives off a blue hue. Babe licked my face, waking me from my last breath. He was immense, just like me, standing twice the height of a normal ox, and three times as wide. To this day, I don't know where he came from, but I was glad to have a friend.

Artist Louis Huard's
depiction of giant
Suttung and the dwarves,
from the 1800s.

Together we ran among the stumps of a forest gone by, destroyed by both our doings (Babe was an ox among ox, hauling tens of thousands of logs for the lumberjacks), happy with our newly found friendship. But the joy was brief, as we began to think about how to fix our devastation.

We concluded there were two things to do. One was to replant the trees, two for every stump we discovered. That we began immediately, gathering pine cones and planting them at a fierce pace. Sadly, we could not keep up with the demand. Something else had to be done.

The only other thing we were good at was intimidation. It wasn't hard for us to strike fear in the eyes of anyone nearby. A simple snarl and a grunt did the job. This talent could be put to good use with the lumber companies, perhaps slowing them down a bit.

The plan worked.

Where I once worked side by side with the lumberjacks, now I toiled against them. Stories started popping up about a crazed giant in the forests, with his demon blue steed, breaking saws and axes like they were toys. Thankfully, they never figured out it was me, Paul Bunyan. I suppose it didn't matter at that point. I was helping my forest grow and replenish itself. Someday I would retire into the forest, filled back in to its original grandness.

As the decades went on, my fight with the lumber companies was winning. They began to replant trees themselves, and only cut so many of the pines down each year. Babe and I were quite comfortable in our young, fresh forest. That is until we smelled smoke.

A battle was brewing, one not with companies, but with campers. Careless campers were starting fires, and not taking care of them. One thing led to another, and I had forest fires starting up every few weeks. It was hard for Babe and I to reach all of them, but we tried our best. This was no way to relax. Something else had to be done.

Babe had a keen sense of smell. He could find a fire in the forest a thousand miles away. Our plan now, was to inspect as many campfires as possible. Sure, I know what you're thinking. That would be impossible. For you, yes. But for Paul Bunyan and Babe the Blue Ox? Never. We were now both well over one hundred years old, and still strong and quick as ever. I don't know if we would live forever, but it sure felt like it.

And instead of intimidating the campers and hikers, we decided to be a bit more covert. Upon arriving at a campfire, we'd quickly survey the situation. If it looked out of control, we'd sneak in and put it out. Many times we'd be spotted (after all, we were giants), and they would scream in terror. But I never heard of a bad story about me and Babe. I guess perhaps that's what happens when you try to do good things. Only the good stories last then.

So the next time you're out in the forests of northern Minnesota, keep a close eye on your fire. Otherwise, Babe and I will be there, lumbering through your campsite to put it out.

HISTORY

TWIT (TUNE WHILE I TYPE)
TIME TO KILL BY GENTLE GIANTS

This, by far, was one of the more fun stories to research and put together. After all, who hasn't heard of Paul Bunyan and Babe the Blue Ox? But I wasn't satisfied with all the legends (and there are dozens). I wanted to find out the truth about who they were.

As with all great legends, they start from facts of some sort. Paul Bunyan, as it turns out, is no different. Historian James Stevens claims that Paul Bunyan has its roots in French Canadian tales, back during the Papineau Rebellion of 1837 (which I'm sure you remember from your Canadian history lessons, ay?), when there was an uprising from England. Paul Bunyan's last name, as it were, stems from the French name Bonyenne or Bonjean, which is sometimes used to mean "Good Grief!" or "Oh My!" During the uprising, a giant, bearded logger-man named Paul Bonjean supposedly helped battle the British. There's also speculation that Paul Bunyan came from the real Big Joe Mufferaw in the Ottawa Valley region, who apparently lived a big life among the logging camps and Canadian forests, chopping down trees.

One other possible basis to the Paul Bunyan legend is with Ti-Jean, or Little John as he was called, a trickster of a man written about in French folklore since the mid-1600s. He apparently traveled to the New World, thriving on the fur-trading business from northern Ontario, Michigan, and Minnesota.

So what lumberjack legends does Paul Bunyan have? Too many to list. But here are just a few:

When Paul Bunyan was born, it took three storks to carry him to his parent's home.

When he was old enough to clap and laugh, the sound broke all the windows in his house.

Paul Bunyan and Babe the Blue Ox dug out the Grand Canyon, by dragging his axe behind him.

Mount Hood was created by Paul Bunyan, by piling rocks on top of his camp fire to put it out.

The Great Lakes were created by Paul Bunyan; he needed a watering hole large enough for Babe to drink from.

The Mississippi River used to be all crooked, until Paul Bunyan grabbed the end of it and pulled it straight.

The 10,000 lakes of Minnesota were created by Babe and Paul Bunyan stomping around.

As you can see, there are many legends, most of which are a bit farfetched. But that's what legendary stories are. And the earliest published versions of these legends are from 1906, from a newspaper reporter of the *Detroit News*, named James MacGillivray.

Today, there are stories and tributes to Paul Bunyan, from east to west in North America. And they continue to grow each year. For Minnesota, the place we most immortalize the giant, is in Bemidji. An eighteen-foot-tall statue of Paul, along with an equally large one of Babe, stands outside a parking lot near Lake Bemidji. Both Paul and Babe were built back in 1937. But the real Paul and Babe are much older.

While most of us don't believe there's a real Paul Bunyan and bluish ox named Babe stealthily traveling through the forests of northern Minnesota, we may be missing the point. To me, what we should be focused on, is if there could be giants living quietly in Minnesota, tucked away deep into the pine and wilderness.

Mythology and folklore are littered with mysterious giants, human-like creatures eight feet tall or more. For centuries we have reported their existence. Well, it's one thing to be told about a sighting of a tall giant, but finding the remains of one—that's different altogether. Below are a few findings, as noted in Robert Lyman's book, *The Forbidden Land.*

In 1856, while plowing a vineyard, villagers in East Wheeling (now West Virginia) unearthed a decayed human skeleton claimed to be ten feet nine inches tall.

Back in 1833, in Lompack Ransho, California, soldiers digging a pit for a powder magazine found a human skeleton twelve feet in length. Furthermore, the giant had a double row of teeth, and was buried with several stone axes, and intricately carved shells and blocks with strange symbols on them.

In Lovelock Cave, seventy miles northeast of Reno Nevada, several mummified remains of red-haired humans were found. They measured over eight feet in length. Local Paiute Indians claim they are from the legends of the giants they called Si-Te-Cahs. Unfortunately, scientists never researched the bones in detail, and many of them were lost. One giant skull from Lovelock is, however, preserved to this day. It's almost one foot tall, and resides in the Humboldt Museum of Winnemucca, Nevada.

There are more discoveries of giants around the country, such as the skeleton found near Brewersville, Indiana in 1975, measuring nine feet eight inches.

In Toledo, Ohio, a large mound was found to contain twenty skeletons with jaws and teeth twice as large as present-day people. And next to each of them was a big bowl with odd hieroglyphic figures.

But what about Minnesota? Did giants ever exist in the land of 10,000 lakes? The answer is undeniably yes.

In Clearwater, Minnesota, seven giant skeletons were found in mounds. Each skull had a strange receding forehead, and complete double row of teeth.

Paul Bunyan and Babe the Blue Ox
in a parking lot off Lake Bemidji.

And what about the six skeletons of enormous size unearthed in Chatfield, Minnesota in 1888, as reported by Jim Brandon in *Weird America*.

According to George M. Eberhart, in his book *Mysterious Creatures: A Guide to Cryptozoology, Volume 2*, there are several places in Minnesota where large skeletons have been excavated. These include: Dresbach, Koronis Lake, LaCrescent, McKinstry Mounds, Moose Island, Pine City, Rainy River, Sauk Rapids, and Warren, Minnesota. So as you can tell, there apparently have been many giants running around the Minnesota area in the past.

But are they running around today? Perhaps. It's hard to say. As of today, I've not heard of any giants roaming down I-35, or living in the Lowry Hill Tunnel. But that doesn't mean they don't exist. We just haven't found the proof yet. Unless we count the players on the Timberwolves basketball team. In ancient times, every player on the team would easily have been considered a giant!

FIELDTRIP

Okay, I admit while I was camping up north, searching for Wendigos, I kept an eye out for Paul Bunyan and Babe the Blue Ox. But only briefly. For obvious reasons, I was way more worried about the Wendigos (refer to the chapter on Wendigos to find out why). And I'm not sure what to think if a Wendigo ran into Paul Bunyan. Who would win? Thoughts of making a movie, *Wendigo versus Paul Bunyan*, flashed through my mind briefly. But only briefly.

The highlight to my searching for Paul Bunyan was visiting Bemidji. I hadn't been there for over three decades, remembering only the pictures of Paul and Babe standing near Lake Bemidji. But if you want a real taste of Paul, you'd have to go to Brainerd, where they have a huge animated statue of Paul, sitting down, talking to you. I remember going there as a kid, around nine years old. My brother and I walked cautiously up to the statue, it's head turning side to side, and I think even his mouth and eyes moved. I thought it was fake, that is until it started talking to me—and said my name!

I'm sure many native Minnesotans and others growing up in nearby states remember that same experience in Brainerd (the original sight was actually in nearby Baxter), with the carnival rides of Paul Bunyan Land. I, in fact, took my own kids there back in 2003, to experience the fright of talking to a giant. It was then that I learned how they got Paul to talk. The trick is to ask nicely (how else would you ask a giant to talk?).

Needless to say, I did not find any roaming giants around Brainerd, Baxter, Bemidji, or anywhere else up north for that matter. But I did find something locally, around Rochester. A sign that Babe the Blue Ox is still around. Sort of. The local Boy Scout Order of the Arrow Lodge uses Babe the Blue Ox on their patch, worn on the uniform. Every time there's a Boy Scout meeting, several scouts have Babe smiling away on the front of their uniforms.

On a more serious note, I did spend some time traveling around Chatfield (just south of Rochester), looking for any evidence of giants (as mentioned in the history section). I wasn't exactly sure where to begin looking for enormous skeletons, and apparently nobody else was either. The few people I dared ask, thought I was nuts (which usually happens when you tell someone you're hunting for monsters). The only information I had, was that the mounds from which the skeletons were unearthed, were located west of Chatfield. If you've never been to Chatfield, let me just say it's not a metropolis. It's a nice small town, one you could get use to living in. But outside of town, there's only miles and miles of farm fields.

Needless to say, I drove around for some time, never really finding the Indian burial mounds. And even if I did, I wasn't planning on digging anything up. Because who knows, a giant could be watching, and not be at all that pleased. And the last thing you want to do is make a giant angry—you'll have a giant of a problem on your hands. Trust me.

MINNESOTA MOTHMAN

"I have never seen a greater monster or miracle in the world than myself."

– Michel de Montaigne
(French Philosopher and Writer. 1533-1592)

I do a lot of driving at night, what with being a traveling salesman. It isn't an easy life, selling industrial strength pressure valves for companies across the Midwest. It's especially not easy, ever since the Mothman creature flew down and attacked me.

I tend to smoke a lot while driving from state to state. Well, I used to that is, when I smoked inside my car. Now, with all the hype about how bad smoking is, I decided to cut back by only smoking outside. Of course the trouble with that is all the increase in stops I was making between Sioux Falls and Chicago. But the stop that nearly killed me (not from the smoking mind you), was the one off Interstate 90 in Stewartville, Minnesota.

I had just left Mankato for the day, filling up the tank of my brand new 2005 Toyota Hybrid Prius. Putting gas in it doesn't happen very often due to its great gas mileage. The trouble was, I'm a big guy (my nickname is Big John), and the Prius is a little car. Don't ask me why I decided to buy it, other than to save a few bucks on gas. But I did what I did, and now I squeeze into it like a greased whale into Jordache jeans.

With gas in my car (and me wedged inside), I headed down Highway 14 to Interstate 35. I would take that south to Interstate 90, which I knew like the back of my hand. I-35 and I-90 are like the bloodlines of the Midwest, allowing you to travel north-south and east-west to just about anywhere. And, as a salesman, that was important. I covered much of the Midwest, from South Dakota to my home state of Illinois, which is where I was heading to that fateful night I ran into the Mothman. Literally.

Well, I can't say that I hit the creature, but I know I would have if I wasn't watching the road closely. By the time I'd hit Albert Lea, it was dark, and I'd already downed three cans of Red Bull. I was alert to say the least – wide-eyed if anything. With my hands firmly gripping the wheel of my little puddle jumper of a car, I continued my way home on I-90.

It wasn't until I drove through Austin that I could tell something was different. Sure, the clouds began to roll in just about sunset, which was nothing unusual around this time in August. The hot sun baked the flat landscape of Southern Minnesota, condensing the air into a humid soup, and sent it upward to form large billowing clouds. Thunderstorms could evolve from nothing, but do lots of damage, including some nasty tornados.

This night I saw those thunderheads forming in the distance. It was an eerie feeling, watching them build into a huge, monster-sized mess ahead of you, knowing you had to drive through them. The worst part was always the front, where the high pressure meets the low pressure. But then that's always the case for trouble—any time two extremes meet, well, there is bound to be issues.

The clouds kept stretching toward me as I drove through the town of Austin. Like I said, there was a weird feeling about these clouds, making the hair on the back of my neck stand on end (and there's a lot there to be standing by the way). But then that could have been due to the strong electromagnetic field an approaching storm can generate. Either way, it was weird.

And then it hit.

The storm front was quick and ferocious, with wind, rain, and large hail pummeling my tiny car from all directions. The cute, white, fluffy clouds above had turned black, with an anger in them only the gods could have created. Thankfully,

Represented depiction of what the Mothman may look like.

me and my putt-putt car took refuge under a nearby bridge. And even more thankfully, the raging storm subsided quickly.

Having been through several of these types of storms in the past, I thought nothing of it. Yet, that creepy feeling had not gone away, even with the clouds departing, leaving a crisp, clear, star-twinkling night. More alarmingly, I kept feeling like there was something darting in and out of the view in my rear mirror. It was the kind of thing you think you see from the corner of your eye, but when you look straight at it, nothing is there. It had started back in Austin, briefly showing up now and then. But now, while coming up on the city of Stewartville, the shadowy figure was flying in my view more frequently.

Thinking I was hallucinating a bit, I pulled off the road on Highway 63, into a nearby Kwik Trip. No, I did not need any gas, but I needed a break. I looked in the mirrors as I pulled into the gas station, and not thinking, began filling my tank. I added a whopping $4.32 in gas, and went inside to pay for it (and also look for some more Red Bull).

Most of the time, I keep to myself. It's not like me to start drilling strangers with questions, especially about weird things. But again, something felt weird, like the air was still electromagnetically charged, keeping my head buzzing and on edge. Of course, it could have been the multiple energy drinks as well. Either way, I found myself (against my own better judgment) asking stupid questions with the attendant at the gas station.

"You have any big bats flying around here?" I asked, in a very natural tone and straight, deadpan face.

The guy looked at me, but made no comment. His face was enough. It had that, "Are you an idiot?" look.

I started making hand gestures, which turned into arm flapping, like I was trying to fly away. "You know, really big flying things. Creatures of some sort."

"Four dollars and thirty-two cents, sir," was all he answered with, although I could have swore I heard the words "psycho" under his breath.

I also noticed the other customers had stopped what they were doing, busily starring at me in a concerned yet Minnesota-nice look.

"I seen what you seen," came a voice from the back of the store. I turned to look and saw an old man dressed in rags hobbling up to the counter. He had to be at least a hundred years old. "The Mothman. It's come back."

Now I had the concerned look, but more of a Chicago, "What the hell is your problem?" look.

The assistant asked for his $4.32 again, which snapped me out of my trance. I paid with a five before turning back to the old man.

Representation of the beady eyes
of the Mothman as it comes at you
while driving down the road.

"What's this?" I asked, half intrigued, yet half annoyed. I was also having trouble concentrating, with a headache throbbing and twisting my mind.

"It came back in the 60s," the old man said while pointing up above. I wasn't sure why he was pointing there, but I looked up, followed by everyone else in the store. He continued. "It'll come again. Always does when there's doom to be."

"You're change, sir," said attendant, shuffling it in his hands. I turned back to get my change, shoving it in my pocket before looking back at the old man. *But he was gone.*

Now I was pointing, pointing to where the old man used to be, looking around at everyone. "Where'd he go?"

It was at this point I realized nobody else apparently saw the old man, which made me even more a freak than I was becoming, what with my crazy questions about large flying creatures. I decided it was in my best interested to quietly shoehorn myself back into my Prius and leave town.

It didn't take long for the flying creature to show itself again. And I was watching for it, seeing some fluttering thing in the distance. Unfortunately, it wasn't far away anymore. It was practically dive bombing me. And that's when I saw its glowing, reflective red eyes.

At first I thought the two red dots were from distant cell phone towers. But as I drove east on I-90, the two red points were moving around, in parallel, and getting bigger. Soon I was mesmerized by them, no longer watching the road. Thankfully, most of I-90 is straight. However I was coming up on a slight curve in the road. Still transfixed on the beady-red eyes, I began to drive off the freeway. Gravel began to spit from behind my wheels. I could sense I was in trouble, heading straight for steep drop off, enough for me to certainly roll my mini-car several times.

The Mothman was now right in front of me and I could see why it was called the Mothman. It was about the size of a person, at least the body was. But behind it, attached to its shoulders, were two gigantic wings, thick as canvas and black as night, fluttering back and forth. At that point I realized I was on a collision course with it. If I didn't react fast, both me and the Mothman would end up at the bottom of the hill in a wicked, twisted metal heap.

I instinctively yanked the steering wheel left, causing my tiny car to immediately swerve that way, narrowly missing the Mothman. Unfortunately for me, I was now heading for the ditch on the other side of the road. Yet, somehow I ended up turning once again, now heading straight on I-90. But not before my cell phone (which I had set on the dashboard earlier) went flying out the window. And, out of the corner of my eye, I thought I saw the Mothman on the left side of my car, pushing it back on the road. *Did the Mothman just save me?*

The entire ordeal only lasted a few seconds. But the memory will be with me for a lifetime. The Mothman's glaring red eyes will haunt me forever. But that's okay, because I think it saved me that night. And you know what else is weird? A month later the I-35 bridge in Minneapolis collapsed. And after doing some research, I learned that the Mothman shows up many times before major disasters.

What's even more alarming, is that I originally had a meeting north of the Cities that day, but missed the invitation due to losing my cell phone during my Mothman episode. I would have been coming down I-35 about the time it collapsed.

Ever since my meeting with the Mothman, I spend more time with my family, and less time worrying about the little things in life. But I also spend a lot more time looking in my rear view mirror as I drive down the road, and wonder if he will ever come back. I hope not. Then again, I believe he saved my life. And I can't help but to think if he helped anyone else change their plans for that fateful day in rush-hour traffic…

History

TWIT (Tune While I Type)

Moth of Many Flames by Spock's Beard

Not knowing the history of the dark, mysterious creature of the night called the Mothman, you might write it off as some silly insect creature, more a nuisance than anything. But the Mothman is much more than that.

It's reported that the Mothman creature was first seen (numerous sightings at the time) in Charleston and Point Pleasant areas of West Virginia from November of 1966 to December 1967. In most cases, the creature is described to be the size of a man, with great wings, and large reflective red eyes. Sometimes the creature is reported to have no head, and beady, red eyes are sunk into its chest. What's interesting, is that it appeared before the deadly collapse of the Silver Bridge (December 15, 1967), which killed forty-six people and two of which were never found.

The next reported sighting happened in June 2007, by an Illinois woman heading home at night, driving through the town of Stewartville, Minnesota on

Actual statue of the Mothman, in Point Pleasant
West Virginia, near the Silver Bridge which
collapsed back in 1967, killing 46 people.

Interstate 90. She noticed a strange winged creature, the size of a man, flying toward her, with red glowing eyes. And, as everyone in the country knows, the Interstate 35 Mississippi River bridge collapsed a month later on August 1st during rush hour.

The structure and deck collapsed into the river, dropping 115 feet down to the river below. With approximately 100 vehicles involved, it was a miracle only thirteen people died (5 of which were never found), compared to the 50-100 estimated initially.

So it seems that the Mothman visited Minnesota, a month before the I-35 bridge collapsed, trying to warn us of an impending doom. The only trouble with this story, is that the witness from Illinois didn't call in (on the show *Coast to Coast*) until a month after the tragedy. I'm not saying the caller didn't actually see the Mothman, but it certainly makes it more difficult to believe in the claim.

It is interesting to note that the Rochester and Stewartville area has had its share of strange occurrences. Such as the Bigfoot sightings in 1968, where it was reported that a large, hairy hominoid was seen south of Highway 52. UFO sightings have also been reported in the area during the same time period. Furthermore, strange, enormous skeletons were reported to have been recovered back in the 1880s, in Chatfield, further southeast of Stewartville.

And to make things even more interesting, we should discuss the odd sightings of a reptilian hominoid creature on Briggs Road near LaCrosse, Wisconsin, about twenty miles from Winona, Minnesota (which is about forty minutes from Stewartville). An old man and his son reported seeing a creature nearly fly into their windshield, staring at them briefly before swooping back into the nighttime sky.

This leads us to one of several possible beliefs about the Mothman, that it is possibly a reptilian species. In particular, they are either aliens from another world, or an ancient race, coming from the dinosaur era, highly advanced and able to easily hide from us. Most of the time that is—unless they're busy running into our windshields, or trying to warn us of an upcoming tragedy.

Regardless, the old man and his son believe something is out there in the Minnesota and Wisconsin area. When they ran into the creature, it made them sick, having to turn off the road and vomit (and remained sick for several days – radioactivity perhaps?). They initially called it the Man Bat creature, that is until they found out about the Mothman. It was about seven feet tall, with dark, leathery wings spanning about twelve feet. It's torso was thin, ribs showing, and it had long skinny legs. Long, sharp claws protruded from its hands and feet, and its pug-nosed face snarled at them, gnashing its sharp rows of teeth. It screamed in a high-pitch wail, then shot up into the air.

It's worth noting that there were several other sightings of strange reptilian creatures that could fly, in and around the LaCrosse area. Investigations have been attempted in the Briggs Road area, but were ended abruptly after investigators became worried about a strange flying creature hovering nearby in the tops of the trees.

And one final report to mention, from October 2006, a man claimed to have seen a huge bird near Stillwater, Minnesota. Some think it could have been a Washington Eagle, which is a gigantic eagle species (as described from John James Audubon in the mid 1800s). The creature was also reported two years earlier by a different individual, but near the same area.

So as you can tell, there are numerous reports of a winged creature in the southeastern area of Minnesota, supposedly the Mothman. It's hard to say if the sightings are fact or fiction, what with no evidence available. But perhaps this is your chance to capture some—spend some time in Stewartville or Rochester, late at night, and listen for the flapping of wings. Giant wings to be exact, with large, reflective red eyes beaming back at you. And don't worry, the creature isn't known for killing anyone—yet.

A MINNESOTA VAMPIRE

*"One thing vampire children are taught is, never run with
a wooden stake."*

– Jack Handy
(American Writer and member of
Saturday Night Live from 1991-2003)

I am Dracula. Or, to be more precise, I am Vladimir the Impaler.

I was once a proud Prince of Romania centuries ago. I have been written about, portrayed as a blood-thirsty killer. While my methods of ruling may have been unorthodox, I assure you they were well needed. The tyrants and unruly kings I had to deal with, required ghastly measures.

You may wonder why I am associated with Minnesota? Simple. There are two individuals focused on my well-being, living in rural area of eastern Minnesota. It has been centuries since I lived of flesh, blood, and bone. But now, through them, I am alive once again.

My spirit, as it were, lives within them. I inhabit the man's body, but only by his choice. It feels good once again to breathe the damp, rain-filled springtime, or the dry, crackling leaves of fall, or the icy, frozen tundra of winter. Minnesota, as it turns out, is very much like my old world back home.

Many have wondered, will I do evil once again? I must state my innocence; there was no evil coming from me. The evil was in the hearts of my enemies, all of which I vanquished with a sharpened pole through the gut, suspended high in the air for all to see. Death was slow and painful for my enemies, sometimes lasting days. And so far, none from this new Midwestern world has crossed my path, seeking my demise. That, I must say, is good for them.

Artist's rendition of
a vampire, complete
with razor sharp
bicuspids.

I am grateful for the couple's generosity; sharing their bodies with my spirit is not done easily. For when I am here, they are not. I could, through my powers, take matters into my own hands in a more permanent fashion. But that is not how I live anymore. I understand this moment back on earth is a gift, an opportunity to live once again. While I still feel anger toward those who condemned me back in my homeland centuries ago, I do not seek retribution here among those who are not guilty. So, people of Minnesota, you are safe.

Another thing I'd like to clarify, is this business with my association to vampires. While I admit I have a taste for blood, I do not claim to be a creature of the dark. Vampires, so it seems, are ruthless, immortal monsters, bent on the destruction of humanity. I am not against humanity, only the ill-fated thoughts some of those among us create. Thoughts that alienate us, dividing us from our true nature, that which is wild and alive.

But I digress. I am here, due to the love this couple has freely given to me. And in turn, I give them love back. They share in my passions and wisdom that I have gained over the centuries.

That is not to say this process has been without pain. For when they hurt, I hurt. Their thoughts and feelings surround me, covering me in a thick, stinging blanket of reality, one not so easily removed. But together we embrace this new life, sharing in our ways, exploring a new awareness, and thankful for what we have.

I am appreciative of the décor in their home. Much of which is medieval, in a Tudor style house, complete with tapestries, stained glass windows, and weapons of my previous time. There are even paintings of me, to help remind myself of what I looked like back then. Which, after centuries of floating as spirit, is helpful. I can remember that I was once a great prince.

I must admit that I find this culture alarming. Not in a negative way, where man is pitted against man. On the contrary, I find this society much too complacent. It is a play full of actors who are no more than just an audience. The action of doing has been replaced by the action of watching. All who sit in their houses, resting comfortably in their chairs, will never see or breathe the real world. And what kind of life is that?

Perhaps, just perhaps, I could change things once again. Maybe I could open the eyes of my hosts, allowing them to see and breathe a true life, one filled with energy, excitement, and danger. It is much too easy to forget how life is lived not in the confines of a cave or house, but on the edge of a cliff or out on the road.

Sadly, it is not for me to decide. Not unless my hosts agree to it, which, I presume would not happen. Nor do I want to take advantage of the situation. It is enough to be alive, through them. I have no desire to upset their lives anymore than I have. They have their own destiny, just as I had chosen mine. Yet, in this afterlife, I seem to have been given a second chance. Am I to spend time seeking my revenge? Or is it for redemption? A difficult decision to say the least. Life, even in spirit form, can be confusing.

So allow me to testify on the behalf of all spirits; we are here. We hear and see you, and some are waiting for their turn to live again. Will you give us that chance? Will you be a host to ancient spirits from afar? Your rewards may be great.

I wonder too, how long I will be with my hosts. And where will I go then? My plan of course is to continue existing among the living through others, willing to open themselves to me. Might that be you someday? Perhaps. You may find yourself alone on a dark sidewalk, illuminated only by the soft glow of the full moon. I may be there in the shadows, waiting for your thoughts to find me, waiting for you to embrace my presence. Then you too can know the power of Vlad the Impaler, you too can know what it is like to be Dracula.

HISTORY

TWIT (TUNE WHILE I TYPE)
A VAMPIRE'S VIEW BY FLOWER KINGS

Let's be honest. Vampires in Minnesota? One would think not. Apparently it's way too cold for them, because I couldn't find very many stories on them. But that doesn't mean they aren't living next door to you unless you see them sunning themselves on a hot summer month. Sure, there's your typical teen chat rooms with self-proclaimed vampire kids, talking through the night about being vampires. Some of them apparently like to drink blood from volunteer donors. Yuk. But from what I can tell, none of them turn into bats and fly around to unsuspecting houses.

Of course, I can't say there aren't any in Minnesota, but if there is, they're just as elusive as the elves (but much taller and with an altogether different diet). Still, we have the couple from Minnesota, as mentioned above in the story, that believe they are possessed by the spirit of the real Dracula. I'm not talking the fancy one in the movies. This is the guy that started it all—Vlad the Impaler.

Vlad was most certainly ahead of his time, sort of having a guerilla warfare attitude, doing whatever it takes to win a war. Like, for instance, impaling your prisoners on giant stakes outside your castle, leaving them to a slow, painful death. Now there's a deterrent if I've ever seen one. And having a name like Dracula doesn't hurt. Back in the 1400s, in Transylvania where he lived, and people translated Dracula to "Son of the Devil" (which is still true nowadays).

Portrait of Vlad Tepes the
Impaler, the original Dracula of
which Irish writer Bram Stroker based
his novel, *Dracula*.

Tens of thousands of innocent people were tortured and impaled by Vlad Dracula, up until he was captured and sent to prison. Yet even in the confines of his cell, he was able to carry out his wicked acts. Guards would enter his room, only to find Vlad with rats he'd captured, with them impaled on sticks around his bed.

So, I'm not sure about you, but I'm thinking Dracula, the real one, is not someone you'd like to be possessed by (unless perhaps your a big fan of Charles Manson, Ed Gein, or maybe Ted Bundy). The movie-based Dracula, however, may be a different story. The power and mystique surrounding the Bela Lugosi Dracula is very interesting. And, in more recent times, the movie *Twilight* has brought on a more romantic twist, and compassionate one, making you really want to care about the blood-thirsty creatures (not to mention werewolves). I read Stephanie Meyer's book, and was pleasantly surprised to find out how much I liked it, once I got past the romantic stuff between the leading girl and the leading vampire.

I did, however, find another vampire sighting in Minnesota. Back in 2006, self-proclaimed vampire Jonathan "The Impaler" Sharkey ran for Governor of the state. And why not? We had just finished with Jesse "The Body" Ventura as Governor, a movie actor and former professional wrestler. It doesn't seem too much of a stretch to hire a vampire, right? Well, apparently vampires don't typically do well in elections (at least not the ones that have come out of their closet).

To me, the story below is more in line with what a Minnesota Vampire would be like:

Susan came back from the woods, holding the side of her neck, and in obvious agony.

"What happened?" I asked, rushing to her from our tent pitched off Lake Itasca.

"Jon, you wouldn't believe it!" Her eyes enlarged to the size of golf balls. "I was attacked by a vampire!"

I tried not to roll my eyes; her imagination always got the best of her. I rubbed her shoulders and said, "It's okay." To humor her, I added, "Let's take a look at the bite." She reluctantly pulled her hand away.

"Whoa." I said, pushing back slightly. "You're right. You do have a bite." At the base of her neck was a deep puncture wound. Unfortunately, there was only one of them. "Wait a minute. Shouldn't a vampire have two fangs?"

"What?" said Susan, now getting groggy and unable to hold her head up.

"Or maybe it broke a tooth." A small amount of blood was oozing down her back from the wound. I looked at her white, pale face, and knew she would pass out any moment. "We'd better get you to a doctor."

That's when I heard it.

It came from somewhere in the darkness of the forest, as the sun set below the horizon. It sounded like a low hum at first, the drone of a motorboat engine, or maybe a large fan.

The sound was getting closer. And that's when I saw it.

The humming had turned to buzzing as the large flying creature came at us. Translucent wings spanning several feet across flapped violently as it hovered nearby. It's long, slender abdomen hung underneath the beating wings, and on its head sprung two large antennae, shifting around as if tasting the air. Most alarming was the needle jutting out, a proboscis several inches long. It was a giant mosquito.

I picked up Susan and desperately ran for the tent, stumbling and tripping as I went. "I think I found your vampire."

At the last second, after diving head first into the tent, I reeled around and lunged for the zipper, dropping it without a moment to spare. The monster mosquito slammed into the tent, it's proboscis stabbing and puncturing the nylon tent easily. Thankfully, that was all the monster could do. It poked and prodded the tent for minutes until finally giving up. That was even after I wasted an entire can of Off, spraying wildly as it stabbed the tent. We waited until morning before packing up and leaving the area, never to return. Not unless we brought along a giant flyswatter and industrial strength can of Off.

To the best of my knowledge, there are no known sightings of giant mosquitoes. Still, this is Minnesota, where unofficially the Mosquito is our state bird. And for those of you who have ever gone tent camping in August, up north, you know that it's not the size of the mosquito that matters—it's the quantity of them. And apparently the sex. Female mosquitoes are the ones that bite. I'll refrain from commenting further, lest I'm backhanded by my wife. Let's just say that some things in nature never change.

One of the more classic drawings of Dracula, similar to what was depicted in the original 1922 vampire movie titled, *Nosferatu.*

Artist's drawing of what a
monster fish might look like –
one needing a new dental plan.

Monster of Mille Lacs

"The "Green-eyed Monster" causes much woe, but the absence of this ugly serpent argues the presence of a corpse whose name is Eros."

- Minna Antrim

I remember watching the movie *Jaws* for the first time (with my legs curled safely up on the theater chair), thinking of how terrifying it must be to swim in the ocean. But we don't have oceans in Minnesota, just lots of lakes—big and small. So there's no sharks around, right? Wrong.

Minnesota has its own kind of man-eating sharks.

I know this for a fact, because I was attacked by one. There's nothing more horrifying than swimming for your life in the crimson tide of your own blood.

I was only ten at the time—old enough to swim on my own, and young enough to believe it. Every summer our family rents a cabin over the Fourth of July on Mille Lacs, one of the biggest lakes in Minnesota by far. With sparklers flickering, and illegal bottle rockets flying overhead, it was a magical moment each season. And Mille Lacs, being quite shallow in many places, was a fantastic lake to swim in. My brother and I could wade out several hundred yards and still only be three feet deep in water. But perhaps its shallowness and our ability to walk far out into the water was the reason the monster fish could easily attack us.

For as long as I could remember, my brother Tommy and I would walk out into the lake, trying to see who could make it the farthest. With Tommy being older by two years, and six inches taller, he always won. At least most of the time. This year, I was determined to beat him, willing to swim over my head. And I would have won, if it wasn't for the killer fish.

"I'm gonna beat you this time Tommy!" I yelled, frantically running into the low crashing waves. With Mille Lacs being so large, there were many times the waves peaked over three feet high. And on windy, stormy afternoons, it wasn't unusual to see five- or six-foot-high swells coming in. Today, however, there was no wind, and virtually no waves.

Tommy smiled and came running after me. "There's no way you're gonna beat me, Joey." With his long legs, he quickly jumped past me, splashing water as he went by. "Can't catch me!"

"Wanna bet?" I said. I kicked it into high gear, pushing myself through the water until I was in up to my neck.

Tommy had stopped, twenty yards in front of me, with the water splashing at his face, smiling the whole time. "Let's see you beat this!"

"I can do it," I replied, trying to dodge the small lapping waves hitting my face. On my tiptoes, I danced my way out to his spot, bobbing up and down to keep my head mostly above water.

"That's cheating," Tommy said. "You're in way over your head!"

Those words couldn't have been truer. But I was a kid—young, dumb, and full of pointless reasons why I should continue further into deeper waters. So that's what I did.

Tommy's smile disappeared as he saw me clearly swimming with my feet no longer anchoring myself to the lake floor. "You... you can swim, right?"

Interestingly enough, I hadn't thought about that too much. Sure, I could tread water when needed, but actually stay afloat for minutes? Doubtful. And at this point, there was only one way to find out. "Of course I can," I replied, with my head bobbing up and down in the water.

Tommy, who in most cases enjoys the things that a big brother typically does, all centered around teasing a little brother like me, could tell things weren't right. He waved his hand to me, with his feet still planted firmly on the lakebed. "Come on. Game's over."

"Maybe," I said, now struggling to keep afloat. "Not until you say I win."

That, of course, was an impossible thing for a big brother to say. In the history of big-brother little-brother battles, it was a rare event when a big brother gave in. Unless of course the little brother was in fact bigger than the big brother. But in this case, Tommy was much bigger than me.

But as I began to slip further into the water, gasping for air, Tommy gave in. "You win, Joey." He waved his hands more, while walking out to meet me. "Come on, let's head back for a snack."

"I win!" I said, several times in between the small waves and struggles to catch my breath, kicking my feet fiercely. And that, I believe, is what caused the monster fish to attack.

I've spent many years wading around shallow waters, feeling the dainty nibbling of a perch, or sunfish, or maybe a small crappie. But this I'm afraid, was something altogether different, and not in the least bit dainty. Whatever hit me, struck with such force that it knocked me down, making me swallow a gallon of water.

"What the—" was all I could hear from Tommy as he raced toward me. By the time he got to me, dark, red blood was drifting outward from my location. *My blood.* I knew this because of the sharp pain that was emanating from my left foot. But I had no time to contemplate much of the situation—I was too busy trying to expel the water from my lungs.

Thankfully, Tommy was there to help. He lifted me up, keeping my head above water, and began pushing us frantically out and to the shoreline. But not before I looked behind us, only to see the monster fish coming back for more.

"Tommy... run..." I tried to say, with water still spewing from my throat, making me cough and heave heavily.

Tommy never looked back, but he knew something was wrong. He doubled his effort, trying hard to move away from the killer fish. By the look of its wake, it must have been five feet long, and had a mouth a foot wide, full of long, sharp gnashing teeth. And I'll never forget the look in its glossy red eyes. Fish really don't have any way to express themselves, but this one had a way to make you believe you were its next meal.

"Musky!" came a yell from nearby. It was my dad, who was paddle-boating with my mom, and could clearly see what was chasing us. Just as the Musky was ready to bite again, my dad threw his lifejacket at it, or at least near enough to spook the fish into halting its attack. With a large flick of the tail, and its head twisting high into the air, it lunged down into the water, never to be seen again.

After an ambulance ride and eleven stitches, I was back in the cabin by nightfall, numb from the terror of what attacked me in the lake, with sparklers flickering through the window, and bottle rockets screeching somewhere overhead. My big brother Tommy, shocked as much as I was, and with a few minor wounds from me scratching him during the assault, sat beside me. We tried playing Monopoly (our usual favorite), but my mind was not in the game. It was still out there on the lake, wondering who the monster fish would attack next...

So most of you would ask, do I swim in lakes anymore? The answer should be obvious. Hell no, I won't go. Not unless I have a waterproof bazooka gun with me, or maybe a Samurai Warrior or two. That Musky was way too big for me to deal with. As for yourself? Well, all I'll say is just be careful the next time you go swimming in a Minnesota lake. There's more than perch and sunfish lurking down below.

HISTORY

TWIT (TUNE WHILE I TYPE)

BE QUICK OR BE DEAD BY IRON MAIDEN

Anyone who's grown up in Minnesota, has probably swam in a lake before. After all, you have your choice of over 10,000 lakes. Some are small, while others are quite large. And with the bigger bodies of water, there are most likely bigger bodies of fish. But big enough to eat you?

The above story is based on several different attacks, from different lakes. But the point to make is that they were in fact attacks. Yes, that's right—fish are attacking people in the lakes of Minnesota. But to the point where they'd swallow you whole, like in the movie *Jaws?* Hardly.

Regardless, a nice-sized Muskie, or Muskellunge, could at least do some damage, ruining your vacation at the cabin off the lake. How about the fourteen-

A hungry shark showing its sharp, dagger-like teeth. There is the potential for Bull sharks in Lake Pepin by swimming up the Mississippi River. Swim Swim… Chomp Chomp.

year-old boy back in 1995, swimming at a public beach on Lake Rebecca, Minnesota. While enjoying the warmth of the sun, and the waves splashing against him, a fish swam up and bit his right hand and wrist. The attack occurred while leaving the water, during a routine safety check requested by the lifeguards on duty. Authorities caught the thirty-eight-inch Muskie and relocated it to another part of the lake.

Of course, I'm thinking, why would they let it go? Isn't it similar to when there are bear attacks—you shoot the bear, so it doesn't get use to the taste of humans. Perhaps now that Muskie will be on the lookout for more dangling hands and feet, hungry to taste once more the flesh and blood of humans.

More recently, in 2007, there was another Muskie attack. A nine-year-old boy was attacked while swimming on a warm summer day in one of the many Minnesota lakes. And it was reported that there was tons of blood (at least that's what the boy saw). The boy was walking out of the lake, in shallow water, when something struck his leg.

He felt the pain immediately, and quickly ran out of the water. Later inspection showed several teeth marks on the heel of his foot.

And what about in 2004, where an eleven-year-old boy was quietly hunting for frogs in the shallow waters of a reed bed. Little did he know, he would soon become the hunted. The boy's nine-year-old sister was with him when the fish attacked. They were wading through only a foot of water on Island Lake, near Moose Lake, when the giant fish began to bite.

The boy's father, nearby on a paddleboat, heard the screaming. He watched as his son began beating the water at something that was creating huge splashes. The big fish (they were not sure if it was a Muskie or a Northern Pike) locked onto the boy's foot, not letting go. Only when the boy reached down to pull the fish off, did it release. But then it bit his hand instead.

In seconds it was over. Terrified by the experience, the boy spent the rest of his vacation in their cabin, inspecting the eleven stitches he had received (not to mention the several dozen cuts). And as far as hunting for frogs, well, he's apparently given that sport up.

Many joke about how the Muskie is known as the Minnesota Jaws, but it's no laughing matter. With Muskie's known to weigh more than thirty pounds, they can easily cause problems for the unsuspecting swimmer—especially the young ones.

But in most cases, they see you and they'll swim away. But if your dangling your feet in the water, or fingers—like a worm, well, I guess they may see it as a free lunch. And with their mouthful of teeth (yes—these fish have some serious teeth), it's not going to feel too good if bitten.

But how big can a Muskie or Northern Pike actually get? Is it possible to see one over a hundred pounds? It's hard to say. But that would be big enough to do some serious damage to your swimming adventures. Currently, however, most records around the country for Muskie (including Minnesota) are somewhere just over fifty pounds, and over four feet in length. Still, those are big fish. Northern Pike are in the same boat (no pun intended), but slightly smaller, topping out at just under fifty pounds.

What's surprising to me, is that the attacks are occurring in shallow water, knee high at best. But then again, that's where most Muskie and Northern Pikes are feeding—in the reed beds, looking for smaller fish. So it makes sense that's where the bites occur. What's troubling is that the shallow water is where the children typically play as well. So no wonder the attacks are mainly on children playing near the shoreline.

The good news is, as far as I've researched, there are no deaths from fish attacks, as in nobody's been eaten by one in a Minnesota lake. That said, there's some pretty big lakes out there, hiding who knows what in them. Historically speaking, there are no man-eating fish in Minnesota (but we won't discuss Lake Superior, which is big enough to contain very large fish—whale size for that matter). But in the future, perhaps we will find bigger fish, topping the scale at over 100 pounds. That, in my opinion, is getting to the size where they could easily become deadly.

I always remember swimming in lakes growing up, always feeling the tickle of the sunfish and bluegills nibbling at your toes. It was cute and harmless. But now, after doing the research for this book, I wear swim shoes. Actually, I've been wearing swim shoes for years, to keep from getting my feet chewed up on rocks and things at the bottom of the lake. Now, well, I wear them to keep my feet from getting chewed up by big fish.

Don't get me wrong. Swimming in Minnesota lakes is awesome. But it's good to limit your risks. Statistically speaking, you probably won't get bit by a big monster fish. But they're out there, and at some point they may be swimming near you, hungry for some worm-looking toes or fingers. So think twice about dangling your feet off the dock, or letting your hands wriggle in the water as you sit in the shallow waters at a beach. You may be a target for a monster fish's next meal. Dum-dum… dum-dum… dum-dum dum-dum dum-dum dum-dum… <queue JAWS theme>

PEPIE THE LAKE MONSTER

"Never say bite me to a Vampire."

– Anonymous

I have to say my childhood memories of Lake Pepin are fond, for the most part. There is one recollection I'd like to forget, though. Which makes sense, being that it involves a monster.

A lake monster, to be precise. Nowadays they call her Pepie, but back in the old days it was just known as the Monster of Lake Pepin. And for good reason. Several times I had confronted it, each time more dangerous than before.

The first incident occurred when I was about eight years old. I had been playing on the beach near the north side of Lake City, towards Frontenac State Park. I was skipping rocks with my two friends, Jason and Devin, on a calm Sunday morning just after sunrise. Jason has a cabin nearby that we'd stay at over the summer. Skipping rocks was a treat on Lake Pepin, as it was normally too choppy with large waves, due to it being over twenty miles long and two miles wide.

"Watch this one!" yelled Devin as he spun a small, flat rock into the water. It skipped seven times before sinking below. "Beat that!"

"Easy," said Jason, over confident as usual. He flipped a rock onto the water, but it was a dud, only skipping two times.

"Ha!" yelled Devin.

Jason, who was nearly twice Devin's size, stomped over to Devin, grabbing his shirt. "Are you laughing at me?"

Devin gulped. "*With* you. I'm laughing *with* you." He looked out to the water, avoiding Jason's gaze. "Nice throw, Jason. I think you, uhm, beat me."

"Sure did," said Jason with a beaming smile as he let go of Devin, dropping him to the sandy shore.

Jason looked at me and said, "Your turn, Robbie." He smashed his fist into his hand and added, "But I'm sure you won't beat me either."

"Probably not," I said while winding up for a massive stone toss. The rock was bigger than it should have been, but I figured I might as well try something different. You get extra points by tossing a large

A drawing of a lake
monster, similar to one
sighted numerous times
in Lake Pepin.

rock, even if it only skips two or three times. In my case, it only skipped once. And when it landed, it hit something poking out of the water—something that shrieked and bellowed loudly when struck.

"What the—" yelled Jason, before backing away from the water in which he was knee deep. The creature, whatever it was, swam only thirty yards away from us.

"It's the monster!" screamed Devin, who was always overly theatrical. In this case, it didn't matter. Seeing a monster's demon-like head rise above the water warranted lots of screaming. Which all of us did while running away from the shoreline, back to Jason's cabin.

Nobody believed us, of course, thinking we made it up for a joke. I began to wonder if it was real myself. *What did I see in the water? What did I hit with a rock?* I wanted to find out more, yet, the strangeness of the event kept me far away from the shoreline for quite some time.

Years later, while fishing with some friends in a small aluminum boat (with next to nothing of a motor and only one oar), I ran into the monster again.

"Pass me the worms," commanded Devin from the front of the boat. "I have a feeling this will be our lucky day. We'll be pulling in a monster of a fish any minute."

I wished I would have listened to what he had said better. Instead, I reached out to him with my hand full of worms for fishing, all the while our twelve foot boat kept bobbing up and down in the three-foot-high waves. It was windy and wavy, but not much more than usual.

I had my line in the water already, complete with bobber, as we drifted toward shoreline on the south end of the lake. It was too deep for an anchor, so we figured we'd just float our way over to the shore at some point. What we didn't figure on, was catching a lake monster.

My fishing pole nearly broke it dropped so fast. "Whoa," was all I could say while trying desperately to hold onto my pole.

"Man!" yelled Devin. "That thing must be huge!"

Then, as suddenly as the attack on my dangling worm down below began, it ended (with my pole in two pieces, minus the fishing line). The attack did, however, continue, but this time *we* were the worm.

Thud... Thud... Thud...

"What's that noise?" asked Devin.

"Dunno," I replied, although somehow I knew what it was. The lake monster. But there was no sense in freaking out Devin. Perhaps it would just go away and leave us alone? Hardly. What fun would that be?

As I expected, the creature from the depths surfaced, with its familiar demon-like head popping out in front of us, and hypnotic red eyes staring us down. This was not a good situation.

"Run!" yelled Devin, oblivious to the fact that we were in a boat. And he nearly started running, except for the fact that the boat was rocking too much for anyone to stand up.

We grabbed the sides of the boat and braced ourselves for more impacts, hoping it wouldn't sink our ship. Thankfully, the lake monster dived below and the pounding on our hull stopped. That was my second run-in with Pepie, but not the last.

The next and final bout with the lake monster came years later, after attending college at Winona State. I met up with some college buddies to do some water skiing on Lake Pepin. I was reluctant at first, being that I hadn't set foot in Lake Pepin since the last time I'd met with Pepie. No sense in trying to make waves. And I didn't want to bring up the fact that I believed in monsters. Or did I? It had been so many years ago, back when I was just a kid. Perhaps it was all just my imagination.

I couldn't have been farther from the truth.

"Your turn, Rob," said Paul while holding out the water skis. "Let's see what you can do."

"No thanks," I said, waiving him off. Getting in a boat was one thing on Lake Pepin. But water skiing? No way.

"What, you've never skied before?" asked Paul. He leaned close to me and whispered while pointing to the two girls that were with. "Come on, it's easy. And I think you'd look pretty cool out there."

I was actually a very good water skier, having gone numerous times in other bodies of water. Just not Lake Pepin. But, to Paul's point, it may be the macho thing to do in front of the girls. Unless of course Pepie showed up. Then I'd be screaming like a girl, which I'm quite sure wouldn't look that good.

And as expected, that's what happened.

I reluctantly agreed to do the skiing, and to my amazement really impressed the girls. They were hooting and hollering from the back of the boat as I launched myself over the wakes, really showing off. I was having so much fun, I dropped a ski and went solo. That, of course, in my cockiness, was the first mistake.

My second mistake was aiming for a large wave to my right. Only it wasn't a wave—it was Pepie. Yes, I had skied myself right into one of its humps, sailing clean over it.

Needless to say, Pepie was not pleased. As for myself, I knew right away I was in big trouble. I looked behind me and saw the hump, along with the other ones, traveling straight for me. I was dead meat, soon to be eaten by a monster.

As Pepie came within a few feet of me, I said my prayers. But for unknown reasons, Pepie swam past me, as if I didn't even exist. Instead, she swam for the boat, determined to knock it out of the water no doubt. And that's exactly what she tried to do.

With one strong whack at the back of the hull, the inboard motor sputtered to a halt. That, of course, meant I would no longer be skimming across the top of the water, but instead be in it. With Pepie. Great. Nothing like swimming with a lake monster.

But at the moment, she was not interested in me. She kept banging on the hull of the boat ferociously, until I could see it cracking. Then, with one last whack from her tail, the boat split in two, sending everyone into the water.

I waited for some time, wondering when Pepie would begin her feast, but it never happened. We watched (among the screaming girls) as the boat sank to the bottom of Lake Pepin. But still no chomping Pepie. Perhaps she was a vegetarian. All I know is that I was lucky to be alive.

To this day I don't go swimming in Lake Pepin. And water skiing? Heck no. I've got better things to do, all of which are done on dry land. And it's not like I believe Pepie is a ferocious killer or anything like that. I think she just likes some peace and quiet now and then. And for us humans to try and keep from waterskiing over her humps.

HISTORY

TWIT (TUNE WHILE I TYPE)

KARN EVIL 9 BY EMERSON, LAKE & PALMER

When people hear the word "lake monster," they immediately think about the Loch Ness Monster (or Nessie as the locals call her), a mysterious creature from across the ocean in the Scottish Highlands. Nobody would ever think that there are lake monsters in the U.S., right? Well, sorry to burst your bubbly ideas, but yes, there are. One such monster is Champy, who lives in Lake Champlain, which borders between Canada's Quebec province, and Vermont and New York on the U.S. side. The other lake monster is much closer to our Minnesota home. And that would be Pepie, the lake monster of Lake Pepin.

Lake Pepin is actually a large opening in the Mississippi River (largest lake on the Mississippi, I might add), and one of the deepest. Spanning over two miles across, and twenty-two miles long (which is surprisingly about the same size as Loch Ness), it's a perfect spot for

A classic lake monster, swimming in the depths of your nearby lake. Or is it? This happens to be a drawing of an Elasmosaurus, a giant prehistoric sea dinosaur from the Late Cretaceous period.

a monster to live. Especially with an abundant supply of fresh water and food (plenty of fish in the lake).

So it's one thing to claim there's a monster in your lake, but it's another thing to have documented eyewitness accounts. Unfortunately, to date, there's no detailed pictures, video, or audio to support any claims. It's all word of mouth, but with a $50,000 reward for hard evidence that Pepie exists, one would think we'll be getting video clips soon enough.

But it's not just a pretty picture that's needed; DNA or some biological evidence is required. Something you can take to the University of Minnesota for analysis. Larry Neilson, local business owner and the one putting up the cash for the award, wants real proof available, something undeniably monsterish. A picture of the monster would in fact work, but it would have to be really, really good. That, of course, may be extremely difficult to do unless your swimming alongside the creature.

Legend has it, the Dakota Native Americans wouldn't travel across Lake Pepin in flimsy thin bark skin canoes. There were sightings apparently centuries back from them, warning others not to travel on the lake. Only if they had a larger, hollowed-out log canoe, would they attempt to navigate across the lake.

The most famous sighting happened back on April 28, 1871. Reported in the *Minnesota Almanac*, published by the Minnesota Historical Society, "a lake monster is seen swimming in Lake Pepin." Giles Hyde and C. Page Bonney, apparently saw a sea monster near Stockholm (located on the Wisconsin side of Lake Pepin), the size of an elephant, swiftly moving through the water.

Schelly Schimbeno, who currently manages the Chickadee Cottage Tea Room and Restaurant off Lake Pepin, remembers her run in with Pepie. "It was 25 years ago probably. My brother and some friends were out in a bay north of town water skiing. And I was in the water and I saw something surface near the boat. It was as long as the boat, which was sixteen feet. It was black, it was ugly, it was long, serpent-like, I would say. I saw something. I'm not going to tell you it's Pepie. But I'm not going to tell you it wasn't."

Back in the early 2000s, Steve Raymond, 57, was fishing with a friend, boating northeast on Lake Pepin to do some pan fishing along the shores near Stockholm, Wisconsin. "Up ahead, I thought I saw a tree, but it wasn't a tree. It was undulating. We got closer, maybe 50 to 75 yards from it, and I saw at least 20 feet of it out of the water. It was greenish, with a cast of yellow." Raymond did take some pictures of the beast, but has since then misplaced them.

Several stories have been told by local fishermen, where they have been attacked while on the water. They would see something splashing near the boat, then hear loud knocks on the hull. Then, several violent back and forth swings would rock the boat, nearly send them to the bottom of Lake Pepin. Some have even claimed to have seen the hypnotic red-eye and demon-like head Pepie supposedly has.

And on July 9, 2008 at 10:00 a.m., a "very large creature" was spotted swimming along the Lake Pepin beach in Lake City, Minnesota. It was estimated that the beast was 30 to 40 feet long, and startled several motorists traveling along Highway 61. Several attempts were made to take pictures of the monster, but it slipped beneath the water too quickly.

In September 2009, Roger Garlitch of Lake City saw something "very large, about 30 feet long" swim along the beach about 20 yards off the shore. And on a moonlight cruise onboard the Pearl (owned and operated by Larry Nielson), several passengers saw something very large swim through the moon's reflection in the calm surface of the lake. Nobody was able to take a picture, as it happened so fast, but many of the passengers swear it was Pepie.

And even Larry Neilson (who is offering the reward) has claimed to see something, possibly Pepie, in the waters of Lake Pepin. "We were the only boat out there. The lake was smooth as glass. We saw a wake about a foot and a half, two feet high, and about two hundred feet long going down the lake. It was very strange. We watched it for quite a while and could not figure out what it might be." It was reported that it had three humps, with one hump being its head.

As you can tell, there are many reported sightings of the beast, or at least something very large in the waters of Lake Pepin. Speaking of which, there is another monster that supposedly lurks at the bottom of the lake. It's the "Mother of all Lake Pepin Clams," a monstrous-sized clam called Clara. She is apparently friends with Pepie, where Pepie ties a rope to Clara and has her water ski around the lake late at night. It's rumored that Ralph Samualson watched this one night off the shores of Lake Pepin, and thought, "If a clam can water ski, why can't a human?" Which of course, was the beginning of waterskiing (Samualson invented the sport at Lake City, the birthplace of Water Skiing).

While it's one thing to speculate that a lake monster lives in Lake Pepin, it's another thing to believe there's giant clams that water ski. It is true, however, that clams that were once harvested in abundance at Lake Pepin, were used to make "Mother of the Pearl" clothing buttons.

But so far, Pepie has become a more famous monster than Clara (hopefully there's no rift between the two of them). Pepie is a huge tourist attraction for Lake City and the area, becoming nationally known (if not internationally). In fact, Heidi Freier, a documentary film director, has spent much of the last year compiling a movie on lake monsters, including the famous Loch Ness, but also doing an expedition to Lake Pepin—hopefully finding evidence of Pepie. As of this writing, they had not found any proof, either to validate the existence of Pepie, or to rule her out. It was interesting, though, that while they scuba-dived in the depths of Lake Pepin, one of the divers saw something huge, and promptly got out of the water, deciding never to return.

In the end, however, I believe each of us has to make a choice on whether or not Pepie is real. Scientifically speaking, the likelihood of a lake monster living in Lake Pepin is next to nothing. But, as it's been noted, there's no proof to state there can't be a lake monster there. And who knows? Maybe there are secret underwater caves in the deeper sections of Lake Pepin, providing plenty of room for a whole family of lake monsters to frolic and play. And that would be a BIG maybe.

I'm not saying there isn't something big down there at the bottom of Lake Pepin. As you'll read in my fieldtrip section, I found interestingly large sonar hits while traversing the lake late at night. There are, in fact big fish out there. The lake sturgeon, a very common fish more than a century ago, can grow to over six feet in length, weighing in at more than 200 pounds. This, could be a very likely candidate for the sightings. Yet since the locks and dams have been implemented on the Mississippi River, the numbers of lake sturgeons has dropped dramatically (although they apparently are on a comeback).

One other possibility, at least when viewing sonar, is large schools of fish. This could also explain some of the huge, mysterious wakes that show up out of nowhere on a calm morning or night. And one final feasible option to explain away the beast, is to conclude that it may be a bull shark. Yes, that's right—there could be sharks swimming in Minnesota (which goes against my story somewhat in Monster of Mille Lacs). Bull sharks have been found hundreds of miles upstream on the Mississippi River, and on other rivers as well. Apparently, a bull shark can handle fresh water (they are normally found in the ocean, or in this case, Gulf of Mexico). And female bull sharks can reach lengths of up to thirteen feet, weighing more than 700 pounds. That, my friends, is a real monster. You may want to think twice about swimming in a river connected to the ocean—or at least make sure you swim wearing chainmail.

So whether you're just trying to get away for the day or weekend to Lake City, visit the birthplace of Laura Ingalls Wilder in Pepin, Wisconsin, see where the tragedy of the Sea Wing steamboat disaster took place in 1890, or want to find out why Father Louis Hennepin gave the lake its name (Lake Pepin translates to "Lake of Tears") in 1860, I believe there's one thing you can do for sure: Watch the water for Pepie. Who knows, you may be able to catch a glimpse. And why not do some swimming? Then, for sure you can pull a tooth from her mouth, or a scale from her tail – that is of course if you don't get eaten first.

FIELDTRIP

I have to say, this was one of the more enjoyable fieldtrips I've done. Who wouldn't want to camp out on a beach all night and watch the stars twinkling above? Or riding around in a boat late at night, enjoying the misty breeze lightly splash in your face? Well, as much as I enjoyed it, I couldn't help but think that there was a monster lurking nearby.

At least that was what the reports stated. And I was bound and determined to find out for sure. As you've read, there are a lot of people claiming to have seen Pepie at Lake Pepin, or at least they've seen something in the water they can't explain. I was hoping that I might be added to that list, and not one of those gone missing in the area due to unexplained phenomena such as lake monsters, Bigfoots, aliens, or a strong, sudden urge to visit the Bahamas in January.

To make this expedition a success, I would need a boat, camping gear, and someone brave enough to come with (not to mention have a boat, camping gear,

The author on his late night expedition in search of
Pepie while camping on the shores of Lake Pepin.

and bravery). Luckily, I happen to have a friend with all three of those things. We shall call him Bill, because, well, that's his name.

With the boat loaded with food, camping gear, and things to hunt Pepie with, we were off. It was a short ride from Rochester to Lake City. Actually, we launched our boat down in Wabasha, with plans to spend some time in Slippery's Bar and Grill (where the movie *Grumpy Old Men* was filmed). But time was running short, and we were anxious to go searching for the monster, and most importantly, the sun was setting. And I've set up enough tents in my life time, in the dark (and in the rain and snow for that matter), to know that it's not fun.

It was only a ten minute boat ride to the south end of Lake Pepin, which was where I wanted to set up base camp. The main reason being, that was the deepest part of the lake. And there was plenty of space to pitch tents on the sandy shoreline. My only concern was whether or not Pepie would be crawling out of the lake to feed on us as a midnight snack. Of course, the skeptic within assured me Pepie did not exist, and we were safe. But then I wondered why we were out there. No, I was sure there was at least a small probability that Pepie was alive and well, swimming somewhere within a few hundred yards of me.

With our tent pitched a few yards from the shoreline, and my trail camera strapped to a nearby tree (ready to snap pictures of Pepie as it climbed out of the water to eat us), we were ready to do some monster hunting. I had a portable sonar device which we mounted (via my arm) on the side of the boat. We also had cameras and video with night-vision available. The sun had retired from the horizon, and we headed out to traverse the deeper regions of the lake.

I didn't want to mention it to Bill (for fear he'd not continue with our search), but I could swear I saw several humps in the water, just before sunset. It happened a couple times, all in the same area. I did mention to him how it looked like waves were occasionally forming out of nothing (it was quite calm by the end of the day), to make it look like humps. But I wasn't completely convinced.

Regardless, we set out in the boat, in the darkness, ready to find Pepie. We focused on the deeper, south end of the lake, thinking it was where Pepie spent most of her time. The sonar turned out to be an excellent device to have with. We could see lots of fish (I'd wished many times that I'd brought my fishing gear with), with many of them quite large. But nothing huge (over 48" is huge, in my opinion). That is until we turned around for our second sweep of the area.

A fish over 100 inches appeared on the screen.

At first, I thought it was an error on the sonar. It might have been, but the fish didn't go away. And several times during our investigation, a large fish would be displayed. I'm not saying it was Pepie, but something big was down there, perhaps a school of fish, or maybe a school of Pepies.

The remainder of the night was uneventful, with the exception of a roaring campfire a few feet from the lapping soft waves of Lake Pepin, and the occasional walk along the shoreline with my night-vision video camera, carefully surveying the calm surface of the lake. The beauty of using video, is that you can always review it later, repeatedly, for any phenomena not seen at the time.

We were up early the next morning (after a fitful sleep, thinking at any moment a lake monster head would come crashing through the door of the tent, and not to mention the coyotes howling all night, and the train coming every hour or so). After a quick breakfast (thought about getting some Pepie Chow – sold at the gift shop in Lake City, but opted for the oatmeal we'd brought instead), we packed up base camp and headed out on the lake once again.

Our plan was to traverse the entire lake, using sonar and eyesight to find Pepie. There had been several sightings in the past, near Maiden Rock on the north side of the lake, so we headed there first. I have to say, there were several times when I'd thought I'd spotted something, but it was most likely the waves. Earlier in the morning, the lake was calm, like a mirror to the sky. But as the morning wore on, the wind picked up, as well as the waves.

It took about an hour to get from one end of the lake to the other, during which time we found no clear evidence of Pepie. I was tempted to get into the water and search, but you would need scuba equipment to do it justice. Plus, because it was late in the season (it snowed several weeks later in October), I didn't want to freeze my butt off. Regardless, we continued north, traveling up near Red Wing, Minnesota, before turning back. And, an hour or so later, we were back on the south end. The entire time we found several possible hits on the sonar, and visual sightings, which I would have to review later.

And, after reviewing my video, trail camera from the night (which is motion sensitive and has infrared lights), and still pictures, I did not find any clear evidence that Pepie exists. Which is obvious, because if I did, I would have collected my $50,000 reward from Larry already! I did however, find a very enjoyable time out on Lake Pepin, camping and relaxing as the gentle waves crashed against the shoreline, the stars brightly twinkled above, and the campfire flickered warmly in the cold, chilly night. The only sign of Pepie we found, was perhaps on the way back to Wabasha, when our motor mysteriously stopped working. We thought perhaps we had hit something – did we run over Pepie? Perhaps. So the next time someone spots her, while they're getting that elusive picture, check to see if there's motor marks on one of those humps. And maybe I'll get to split some of that reward money.

RICHFIELD SHADOW CREATURES

"Anger is the enemy of non-violence and pride is a monster that swallows it up."

– Mohandas Gandhi

Ever been watching TV, and noticed something moving out of the corner of your eye, and found yourself wondering what it is? And you know there's nothing there? I've noticed it many times. Except I don't wonder about it anymore. I know exactly what it is.

It's the Shadow People.

My mom would always say, "Susie, it's just your imagination getting a little too active." Sorry, but these creatures are real, Mom. They're scary and nearly impossible to see, other than just a dark mass shifting around out of your normal eyesight. I didn't believe in them at first. But after living with them for years, I became a firm believer.

It all started back when I was young, around six years old. I can remember sitting at the kitchen table in our house in Richfield, eating breakfast. Mom would go down the hallway to do laundry, leaving me alone. That's when they usually showed up.

And it's not like they just magically appear right in front of you. No, they are much sneakier than that. The only time you can see them is through the corner of your eye. You have to not be looking at them directly, using your peripheral vision.

At first it was fascinating, all this movement of dark, shadowy figures running between rooms in the old house, or darting down the hallway. I could deal with all that stuff just fine. But when they started showing up in my room before bedtime, well, that was too much.

Let's just say I did a lot of screaming in those days, calling for Mom every five minutes, until we were both blue in the face. But she was patient with me and my shadow-phobia, allowing me to drift off to sleep with her by my side.

That was fine when I was six, but at age thirteen, Mom figured I had to deal with shadows on my own. That, I'm afraid, was poor advise.

I tried confronting the elusive monsters, calling out to them right after spotting their movement. It did no good. I was more angry than

scared at the time, mad at their intrusion into my life. After all, it was my bedroom, and they were not invited guests.

Bored with yelling at them, I tried setting traps out to catch them. But how do you catch a shadow you ask? Easy. You use light—lots of light. You see, I learned they come from shadows, and must go to shadows. If you remove all the darkness in your home, they can't show up. Pretty cool, huh?

But they were not amused with my plan.

Oddly enough, the lights in the house began to malfunction. So much so, that on some evenings (when my parents were gone of course), all the lights would go out. At first I was angry, being that the TV was out too. Then, as I heard rustling in the blackness of the living room, and a light wind (even though the windows were closed), I curled my feet up underneath me on the couch. *Were the Shadow People here?* In the darkness, they are everywhere.

A scream erupted from my mouth, panicking at all the darkness surrounding me. But as soon as I inhaled for another scream, the lights came back on. *Were they playing with me?*

The creatures were not always scary. Sometimes they were helpful. On several occasions, one of us in the family would leave something out, lying on the floor. We'd head out for an errand, or to soccer practice. When we returned, the item would be put back in its rightful place. Nobody paid much attention to the incidents, but I did. I knew it was the work of the Shadow People.

Going into the basement was never a positive experience. The stairs creaked as you walked down into the dimly lit area. By the fourth step you could feel the energy of someone else down there—some*thing* else around you.

I tried to convince my little brother, Jimmy, to come down with me, but he knew better than that. He was more afraid of the little dark shadows than I was. Especially since he got caught down there with the lights going off. He screamed and screamed until we came down to get him. He never explained what had happened to him down there, but he didn't have to. The same thing happened to me, in my own bedroom.

Artist's rendition of an eerie looking shadow face, sometimes found staring at you from the corner of your eye. Or worse yet, staring from the foot of your bed while you sleep at night.

It was months after Jimmy's episode with the frightful shadows. I had almost forgotten that he had trouble with them. It was a Sunday night; we were all getting ready for bed, to start a new week the next morning. I was excited, knowing Monday was cheerleading tryouts. I wanted a good night's rest, to make sure I had the energy to do the routines. Unfortunately, the Shadow People had other ideas.

Once the lights went out, I immediately knew something was wrong. I had a night light on in the corner of my room, and could see things fluttering back and forth. Also, the light shining in from the half open door would occasionally get blocked out. Something was definitely moving around in my room.

Now shadows and wind and fluttering noises are things I came to deal with over the years. As long as they kept their distance, I was fine.

But they didn't.

Just as I was about to fall asleep, I felt something brush the blanket by my foot. I turned to look, but of course saw nothing. Seconds later, I felt the same thing on my other foot. This time, however, I saw something. It was black, as expected, but tall; not like the other little shadows running around. *Perhaps this was the leader of the pack?*

You know how in your dreams, you try to run away from a monster, and you can't? Well, this was what happened to me, only it was real. And I wasn't trying to run, I just wanted to scream. But nothing came out but a raspy, crackling breath.

Shadow hands continued to touch my legs through the blanket, all the while I lay there, unmoving, unable to do anything. I was for the most part in a catatonic state, a self-induced paralysis. There was nothing for me to do but lay there and whisper dry screams. It was the most horrible moment of my life.

Thankfully, my little brother Jimmy entered my room, or at least tried to. The door slammed shut as he poked his head in, nearly breaking his tiny nose. But that didn't stop Jimmy. He pounded on the door, twisting the handle as best he could, until finally it opened. He raced in, flashlight shining like Excalibur, sending the Shadow People back to their own dark domain.

My parents were right behind Jimmy, worried about the pounding, and now the screaming that was finally set free from my lungs. I tried to explain to them about the shadowy figures always running through the house, but they wouldn't listen (other than Jimmy, who know all too well). I didn't mind though, Jimmy and I would take care of each other. We made sure we slept with flashlights, and never went down into the basement alone.

So you see, we grew up in a house with Shadow People, but we didn't let them get to us. Well, at least not in the physical sense. To this day, as I curl up in bed for a long, peaceful night's sleep, my hand gently taps the flashlight underneath my pillow, and I am comforted knowing I can readily vanquish any evil pursuit of the dreaded Shadow People.

HISTORY

TWIT (TUNE WHILE I TYPE)
SHADOWS IN THE RAIN BY STING

If you've followed the paranormal scene at all, I'm sure you're familiar with shadow creatures. They're also called shadow figures, shadow people, shadow men, etc. Pretty much anything starting with the word shadow.

And really, the description most people give you is, well, shadowy. There's no real concrete definition to what they look like. Just a black, shadowy, three-dimensional moving mass; almost like a thick, black, bag of smoke swiftly running around. They can be tall, short, wide, thin, thick—just about anything as long as it's dark and shadow-like.

The other interesting part of dealing with shadow creatures, is that you can typically never see them straight on. You have to turn, and look using your peripheral vision. Or, if you're staring into a room, you can sort of concentrate on the corners, not really looking at them directly, but sort of seeing them at the very edge of your vision. That's when they are most easily seen.

I have to admit, I've seen a few shadow people. To be more exact, I've seen dark shapes at the corner of my eye. Are they monsters lurking in the room around me? Perhaps. But so far, they haven't bothered to introduce themselves. Not that I'm entirely sure I want that to happen. Still, it's interesting to note that there's something there—I'm just not sure what it is.

I've also noticed them on the ceiling, hovering up high late at night while I lay awake in bed. It's sort of odd, but I can see floating blobs of blackness somewhere above me as I peer into my room with the lights off. Again, I can't say it's shadow figures, waiting for me to sleep, but I can't deny I'm seeing something. Most likely it's a trick the eyes are playing on me; the combination of low lighting, tiredness, and one too many glasses of wine no doubt.

Seriously though, there are people who swear that the shadow people are real. And there are a number of pictures and video capturing the stealthy figures. The following are a few (of many) accounts in Minnesota of people confronting the mysterious shadow creatures.

Several years ago, a young man was sitting in his room, watching television, when in the reflection of the screen, saw some shadow dart across the room behind him. This happened several times, but seemed to disappear for several years. Then, out of nowhere, the

A drawing of a shadow figure,
similar to ones that can be found
swiftly moving around your house
in the dead of night.

shadows returned. He was looking at where the wall meets the ceiling in his room, and a strange dark mass crept into a crack between the wall and ceiling, yet there was no crack. A few days later, he reported seeing the creature with his friend during the day, scurry across the street as they rode their bikes late in the evening. Since then, he has not seen the shadow figures, but is still curious to know what they are.

Another person, a woman from Richfield, Minnesota back in the 1980s to 1990s, reports seeing shadow creatures several times when she was young. She lived with her mom in a two-bedroom rental duplex, which seemed to be terribly haunted. It felt as though there was always someone watching them, especially when they went down into the basement – that was the most terrifying experience. Well, almost. The worse was laying in her bed, feeling like someone was sitting at the end, rubbing her legs. The room would grow cold, and she was able to see her breath. The hairs on her neck would stand on end, until the creature would leave. Things in the house would get lost, or misplaced, only to be found later in a different unexpected location. She suspected it was the shadow people for some time, but it wasn't until she was a teenager that she saw them, late at night, hovering in the corner of rooms (especially her bedroom), or running quickly down the hallway.

Another report comes from a man living in St. Paul, Minnesota, back in 1999 to 2000 – a house on Sycamore Street, with a unique basement apartment used for truck drivers to rest at (alongside a space in the basement where the man rented), and upstairs was a rental place (although it wasn't rented out at the time). The house was located near a huge cemetery, rumored to be called "Angel of Death." As far as the shadow people sightings are concerned, the man saw them while watching TV late at night. He suddenly started to see his breath as the room turned chilly, even though it was summer and there was no air conditioning in the apartment. Then, out of nowhere, a hovering dark mass appeared. He believes the shadow creature was a woman, or at least was at one time, based on the smell of perfume. The figure walked right through the wall that was on the same side as the cemetery. The experience totally freaked him out and he left immediately, not returning until the next day (I'm surprised he even came back!).

The man brought his friend over, to play video games and hang out for a while that evening. At just after 10 p.m. the room began to get cold, enough that they could see their breath. Then that same shadowy lady with the perfume smell came through the wall next to the cemetery. She was quickly followed by two strange shadowy figures, floating right by the man and his friend. But only for a moment. The three shadow people all jumped into the friend's body, at which point the friend starting acting really bizarre, pleading that he needed to move into the basement. The man convinced his friend to go outside and talk about it. Once outside on the driveway, the three shadow creatures sprang from the friend's body, floating away toward the cemetery, and never returned.

Another story comes from Ely, Minnesota, where a family in an old house had a lot of unexplained phenomena happen. Apparently, a man lived there before them in the house, sadly committing suicide. But he seems to still be living there, in some shadowy form. Strange things happen almost every day – like televisions being turned on without anyone around, or dryer doors being slammed shut by themselves. The family dog, Boots, would sometimes start acting really weird, whimpering and growling at nothing. The family would check the house for anything strange, and occasionally find a shadowy creature standing in a room as they turned around to look. But as they focused more intently, the figure would disappear.

A man from Jordan apparently has experienced seeing shadow people, as reported in October 2008. He has lived in the area for several years, traveling along Highway 169 quite often. And many times, he has seen strange, shadowy figures around dusk, walking along the railroad tracks as he drives by between Chaska and Jordan. He originally thought his eyes might be playing tricks on him, perhaps seeing bushes, patches of tall grass, or cedar trees. But it happened too many times to be that. In particular, he stopped on several occasions to watch, and could clearly see that there were no bushes in the way. The dark masses were floating, just above the track, wandering parallel to the iron rails. He didn't bother mentioning it to anyone, until another man he'd met recently talked about seeing shadow creatures walking along the railroad tracks between Jordan and Belle Plaine – exactly like he'd seen. The culmination to the man's experiences, happened just months ago, when he ran right into a shadow figure, past the intersection of highway 41 and 78. He had his headlights on and could clearly see the dark mass walking across the street.

And here's one of my favorites from Minnesota, the classic shadow-figure-in-the-bedroom-at-night story:

A woman claims to have been visited numerous times by shadow creatures while growing up. She would always ask her parents to leave the room of her bedroom door open, so that she wouldn't get scared. Unfortunately, that's where she saw the shadow figures, "silhouettes darker than the darkness" – walking in slow motion back and forth in the hallway outside while she tried to sleep. She was never afraid of them, and learned to accept them in their house. And when she'd need a drink of water, having to go to her parent's bedroom, she'd walk out into the hallway, getting in line with the parade of shadows, waiting her turn to jump out of line to her parent's room. She dismissed the events for several years, until she talked with her sister, who also said she experienced the same thing. And years later, she confronted her mom about the ordeal, who also agreed that it happened to her when she was young.

There are numerous other cases reported, like the man in Stacy, Minnesota who had the shadow men visiting him in his basement when he slept there with his family (with strange, mysterious things happening to their baby in the crib), or the man in St. Paul who to this day still sees shadow people all the time. He believes everyone has seen them at some point in their lives, but it's hard to recognize them, being they usually can only be seen with peripheral vision, and only when they are moving.

Like it or not, many people have encountered these interesting shadows. While they could be considered ghosts or spirits, they could also possibly be creatures of some sort, meaning they're not stuck in the spiritual plane, and are able to move freely among us. That is, when they want to. Whether it's episodes of *Ghost Hunter, Paranormal State, Ghost Adventures,* or *Ghost Lab,* there seems to be something going on with shadows mysteriously moving around. And with evidence captured on the above mentioned shows, with real video showing shadow people, it's hard to refute the claims. But the best thing to do, is sit in a room at home with the lights way down low, and watch things out of the corner of your eyes. And if possible, have a camera recording your little mini-investigation. And maybe then you'll have the evidence we need, to further prove to the world that the shadow people are real. That is if they don't terrorize you and take you away to their own demonic dimension.

Mutant frog run amuck. An artist's rendition of what an extremely mutated frog might end up becoming. That's one frog a princess shouldn't kiss.

MUTANT CREATURES OF LE SUEUR

"I can see every monster as they come in."

- Truman Capote
(American Writer, Novelist and Playwright, 1924-1984)

It was supposed to be a normal day. I had done these nature field trips with the students many times before. But this time, with what we found, terrified us all.

I've been a teacher at the New Country School in Henderson for years. Being a small town environment, it's typical when things are simple and normal. One of the highlights of the school year is doing field trips, either to the Twin Cities up north, or down south along Highway 169 to Mankato. In some cases, weather permitting, we'll make quick trips outside around the area, to explore nature. What I didn't expect, was to find mutants in the marshlands.

The nature hikes were one of my personal favorites. It got the students and me outdoors into the fresh air, to experience the natural world firsthand. There was something relaxing, yet exciting about the walk through the tall grass and marshlands of the area. And every year we'd make observations, record measurements, and take specimens back to research later. This year, however, we got more than what we bargained for.

Mutant creatures from the marshlands.

Yes, that's right. You heard me. We found mutants in our backyards, complete with three legs, or three arms, or even three eyes. It was like aliens had landed. The only trouble was that I knew what they were, or what they were supposed to be – frogs.

After the screaming and screeching of how gross the frogs looked (and there were a lot of them mutated into strange creatures), we decided to take a few back to the school. Several times I wondered if we were doing the right thing. After all, if the frogs had become mutants, what else might be in the area? Worse yet, were *we* being slowly contaminated over the years by some invisible force?

The scientist in me won out, and we quickly grabbed some sample frogs. The students were excited, yet confused. They kept asking me why they were mutated. I didn't have any answers. Then fear struck them, as they began to ask if they themselves were going to become mutated. Honestly, I didn't have an answer for that either, which alarmed me the most.

That night, I hardly slept, tossing and turning with fitful dreams of mutant aliens coming to terrorize our little city of Henderson. When I awoke, I knew it was a dream, yet it still bothered me. Not about any aliens coming to get us, but about what caused the mutation. I had to find an answer, if anything, for the students.

After several days of research, I came to the conclusion that this was way over my head. And for the safety of the students (and the people of Henderson), I decided to contact the authorities. Especially since I was beginning to feel nauseous. *Was I the next mutant?* I was having nightmares, with the people of Henderson as well as myself growing extra arms, legs, eyes—you name it. Perhaps we were the beginning of an epidemic, with mutations spreading across the country and eventually to the world.

It didn't take long before the news hit the national scene. After all, it wasn't everyday a teacher from a small town reported they'd found mutant creatures. That is until I started the trend. Within weeks, mutant frogs were being reported everywhere, and not just in the Le Sueur area. This had become nationwide, yet Minnesota still had the most reported cases.

Soon the Minnesota Pollution Control Agency and the National Institute of Environmental Health Sciences were involved, eagerly busy trying to find out what was going on. Was it the water? Was it the air? How about any radiation leaks? And what if it was the start of an alien invasion? Months went by with no answers. In the mean time, the students continued to wonder. As did I.

For the most part, the mutations stayed within the frog genus. But there were additional reports, stating that other creatures were affected, such as dragonflies. But what really concerned me was how the state and federal governments were involved, yet they could not find any answers. There was no smoking gun to this mystery. For all we knew, human babies being born would soon start to show the mutations.

That was the real question—how far did the mutations go? And when would it end? For several years we continued to find many of the mutated frogs. At one point it seemed like there were more mutated frogs than regular ones.

Then, after only a few years, the research and analysis by the government mysteriously ended. Budget cuts were blamed for the reason why nobody was looking into the mutations. Or perhaps it was something different? A cover up? Maybe there were aliens involved?

These were many of the questions my students would ask, and once again, I still had no answers for them. The number of mutations over the years had died down, but no one knows why. It's still a mystery, one that still needs more investigating. While my health is still good (as well as the people living in Henderson), I continue to research, hoping to find an answer. I just hope I don't wake up one morning from another nightmare, stretching and rubbing my eyes—all three of them.

HISTORY

TWIT (TUNE WHILE I TYPE)
FROGS WITH DIRTY LITTLE LIPS BY FRANK ZAPPA

The above story is based on the events that occurred in the mid to late 1990s. It started originally in Granite Falls, Minnesota, in 1993, where abnormal mutated frogs were found. But it wasn't until 1995, when the students and teacher from New Country School in Le Sueur, Minnesota found large numbers of deformed frogs. The mutations were found within a wetland area near Henderson. By the end of 1995, numerous findings were reported all through the Minnesota River Valley.

In the following years, the Minnesota Pollution Control Agency (MPCA) got involved, interested in finding out what was causing the mutations, not to mention what the extent of the abnormalities were. The National Institute of Environmental Health Sciences also investigated the issue. And, after years of study, the exact cause of the mutations is still unknown. That, in my opinion, is the most alarming factor.

They've narrowed it down to several possibilities: chemicals, parasites, or ultraviolet radiation. What's important to note, however, is that the mutations for the most part have remained within the frog population. The only exception was with dragon flies. So for now, there is no outbreak expected, spreading to humans and causing us to mutate. Or is there? It's difficult to guarantee anything, if the state and federal governments can't determine the cause. But historically the mutations have not branched out to other organisms. At least not that anyone is aware of.

And because we still do not know what is causing the malformations, we don't know the source of the problem. Most scientists speculate that the trouble is in the water, yet a multitude of tests do not show anything overly alarming. Sure, pesticides are there (from the nearby farm fields), and other pollutants, but not to any severe degree. And the culprit to the mutations does not necessarily have to be man-made. It could still be something natural, such as an increase in ultraviolet radiation (which could indirectly be a reflection of global warming, with the depletion of the ozone layer).

So how many places have the mutated amphibians been found? By 1996, thirty-five states in the U.S. had reported them, along with three provinces in Canada. But what's most alarming, is that within Minnesota alone, 87 counties reported the mutations. Could this

Artist's depiction of a mutated human,
growing an extra eye and mouth.

mean Minnesota is more affected? Possibly. I would bet that it has more to do with an increased public awareness in Minnesota. Still, it makes you wonder, is there something happening to the prairielands of Minnesota? And what's next, the forests and cities?

Another item to point out, is that biologists haven't just begun looking at frogs in the past few years. They've been studying them for over 40 years, surveying frog populations and reporting on them. To date, they have never seen this kind of mutation happening, to this extent. It is apparently a recent phenomenon for Minnesota. That, to me, doesn't sound like a good thing. It means that the true affects may not show up in other animals for years (including humans).

It's one thing to see a few deformed frogs here or there, but there are a lot of them in this case. And the mutations appear to cover every inch of the amphibian's body. In some cases the frogs have extra arms and legs, or none at all. Or they will not have eyes (or too many eyes). And the limbs may end up with little to no muscles, or no skin. Internally, the frogs have problems as well. Digestive, reproductive, and urinary organs can be mutated too. The pictures of these frogs (which you can Google for on "Minnesota Mutant Frogs") is scary, to say the least. Especially when you think about whether it will start to affect other animals, or humans.

In most cases, the Northern Leopard Frog is the species that seems to be the most affected. Others are the wood frogs, green frogs, mink frogs, gray tree frogs, and American toads. Overall, nearly fifty percent of frog species are affected to some extent. And if we look at North America as a whole, other frogs are in trouble too. Such as bullfrogs, Pacific tree frogs, long-toed salamanders, tiger salamanders, and spotted salamanders. And let's not forget the dragonflies – they too are apparently becoming mutated.

The frogs that are becoming mutated are being found typically in rural wetlands, marshlands or ponds, depending on the species. What's interesting to note, is that there are mutated frogs also being found in urban town areas, so there's no clear pattern to the type of location they are found, or geographically where they are occurring.

One of the most obvious questions asked through all of this, is whether the water in the area is safe to drink. Standard drinking-water

A picture of an actual mutated frog, showing a third rear leg. All the better to hop with I suppose.

tests have been done, collecting water from numerous sites, but nothing is ever found. More detailed tests have been done, but according to MPCA, it will take some time to determine to what degree the water would affect humans. But as it stands, there is no evidence that water is unsafe for humans.

Unfortunately, funding for the study of these mutant frogs at the Minnesota Pollution Control Agency (MPCA) ended in July 2001. Since that time, little to no work has been done in Minnesota, although an effort continues in other parts of the country. I found it odd that the funding mysteriously stopped, only a few years after it began. Particularly when no root cause was determined. I'm not sure about you, but I would prefer to better understand why animals are growing extra legs and eyes, especially when it's in my own backyard.

And I do mean my own backyard. A nine-year-old girl from Stewartville, Minnesota found a five-legged frog, with twenty-three toes on it. Three of the legs appear to be normal, but a fourth one has another leg growing off it, and three feet attached. Being that I live in Rochester (with Stewartville just to the south), it doesn't make me feel too comfortable, knowing there are mutant frogs right next door.

After researching and writing about the mutant frogs, it's obvious they would not be categorized as strange monsters. Strange, yes. But monsters? Hardly. What I'd like everyone to take away from this chapter are two things. One, that there is the potential for other animals to become mutated, larger ones that could in fact become monstrous. As indicated before, if frogs are somehow being mutated, what's to stop this from happening to other animals? Who's to say there aren't mutant coyotes now on the loose? Or mutant squirrels, wreaking havoc on the acorn population across Minnesota. And I'd hate to think what would happen if a Loon went berserk...

Seriously though, the second thing to take away from this chapter is that perhaps *we* might be the monsters. If the root cause of the mutant frogs turns out to be man-made, well, then I guess we are the monsters for letting it happen. Hopefully, by reading this chapter you will do a little more research on your own, and maybe send an email to your representative, asking about the mutant frogs in Minnesota. And maybe, just maybe, we can prevent a more serious mutation from occurring – something that may not appear for decades, and in the human population. But for now, I guess we're safe, right? And I'll keep an eye on my fingers while I type – just to make sure I don't grow any new ones.

ST. CROIX HOOP SNAKE

"Fantasy, abandoned by reason, produces impossible monsters; united with it, she is the mother of the arts and the origin of marvels."

- Goya
(Spanish artist, 1746-1828)

Most people are afraid of snakes. They slither across your path on a midday hike, or surprise you from under a rhubarb leaf in your garden. Some even come rolling at you break-neck speed, ready to stab you with their venomous tail.

That's what happened to me.

I was out visiting a friend of mine, Josh, at his house in Stillwater, along Arcola Trail facing the St. Croix River. I'd grown up in the area, attending Stillwater Area High School, and we'd always talked about the Hoop Snake. Every time we snuck down to the St. Croix to swim (against our better judgment, in the fast-moving river water), one of us eventually screamed, "Hoop Snake!" making the other run fast away. We'd end up back at his house laughing about it over Mountain Dews and Doritos for the rest of the day.

We'd heard about them from Josh's grandpa, telling us stories about his run-ins with the Hoop Snake, when he was our age.

"Those Hoop Snakes," he'd say while reclining in the rocking chair off the front porch, fanning himself with the day's newspaper on the hot sunny afternoon. "Those Hoop Snakes," he'd repeat, "were everywhere back in my days. Couldn't hardly turn up a rock without finding one."

"Did you ever catch one?" asked Josh, eyes beaming with excitement. He pointed to me. "Jimmy here would like to see one!"

"Ha!" laughed Grandpa, "Catch one!" He'd slap his knee, then sip on more iced tea. "You don't catch them – they catch you!" He always leaned forward, all wide-eyed when he said that. Holding up his finger he'd add, "The tip of his tail was about the size of my finger, only sharp like a needle at the end. You didn't want to mess with the back end of a Hoop Snake. Venomous too." Then he'd poke us in the ribs with his finger and yell, "Gotchya!"

"It must have been difficult to run around and play, or swim in the St. Croix River," I would say.

"Most definitely," said Josh's grandpa, now leaning back and rocking in a slow, steady motion. "If you weren't careful, you'd end up deader than a goose froze to the river in January!" He paused a moment from his rocking to add, "In fact, there's been a few boys that have gone missing over the years. Let's make sure you two aren't added to the list." He smiled, then ruffled his newspaper and began reading it for the tenth time that day.

Josh's grandpa, along with the stories he'd tell, were gone now. But the memories remained. Now Josh and I are in our twenties, with families starting of our own. We'd tell others the stories about the Hoop Snake, knowing they were just that – stories. Right? Well, not exactly.

As I was saying, we ran into one while visiting with Josh and his family. We decided it would be fun for the two of us to head down to the St. Croix and dip our toes in it – just like the old days.

"Race you to the river!" said Josh as he darted ahead of me along the winding path to the shoreline.

"Not if I can help it!" I said, running barefoot at break-neck speed, dodging rocks and fallen twigs along the way. But Josh was the track star, and could easily out sprint me. Or would have, if it wasn't for something sunning itself on the path in front of us in the late afternoon sun.

"What the—" yelled Josh as he came to a skidding halt. I nearly barreled over him, sending us both at the thing coiled up in a perfect circle, with its head gently biting its tail.

"Is that what I think it is?" I asked nervously and out of breath.

Josh shook his head. "Nah. It's just a… snake."

I jabbed Josh in the ribs, smiling. "Could be a Hoop Snake?"

"Why don't you go find out," replied Josh as he swung around and pushed me right at it.

"Whoa!" I said, barely finding my balance. I shifted forward, now only a few feet from the snake. I could see it was clearly something other than your typical small Garter snake, but could still possibly be a larger snake like a Fox or Bull. It was similar to a Rattler snake, minus the rattles. Although I couldn't get a good look at its tail as it was buried in its mouth. And what was really strange, was that it was coiled in a perfect circle. "Just a snake," I said with a half smile, trying to convince myself.

As if trying to defend its territory, the snake twitched, then flipped on its side, in a rigid circular formation, its teeth still firmly mounted on its tail.

It was on edge, facing me like a scaly bicycle wheel, ready to roll.

"Okay, now that's weird," said Josh while taking a step backward.

The snake began to roll toward us. Dust from the trail kicked up behind it.

"Weird or not," I said while slowly backing down the hill toward Josh's house, "I'm out of here!"

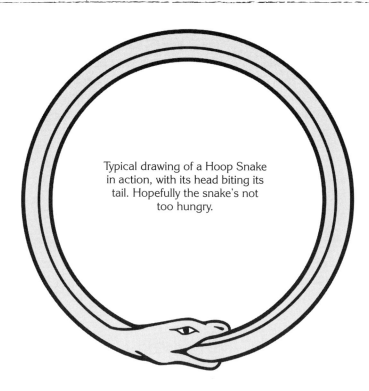

Typical drawing of a Hoop Snake in action, with its head biting its tail. Hopefully the snake's not too hungry.

And the chase was on. Snake versus Man. Which would win? Well, being that I'm writing this story, man obviously won. But that was a run I'll never forget.

Just like when we were young, after someone yelled "Hoop Snake!" we ran and ran, never looking back. But this time it was real, and I knew it was there. Somehow it was able to hiss while rolling and holding onto its tail. And according to my quick calculations, the snake would get us in a matter of seconds, being that we were several hundred yards from the safety of Josh's house.

"Heading… up… the hill!" Josh yelled from way in front of me (track star, remember?) as he twisted right and began climbing the hill. It was a gutsy move, what with us now going farther away from his house, but it seemed to be working.

Then, of course, I said the infamous words that should never be said while being chased by a monster. "I think we're gonna make it!"

The Hoop Snake clearly was losing momentum as I quickly glanced back. What I didn't realize was that there were two more at the top of the hill, ready to roll down and stab us with their venomous tails.

It must have been a whole family of them. I wondered briefly what a family of snakes did for enjoyment. Obviously chasing stupid humans was one of them. And the prize at the end was administering a pointy painful death. Not if I could help it.

Josh, who was faster, was already only a few feet from them. So there we were—snakes in front, and a snake in back. What to do? Well, there was only one thing I could think of to do. It made no sense whatsoever, but I did it anyway.

"Roll!" I yelled while dropping to the ground and rolling back down the hill.

"Huh?" said Josh. He watched me roll down the hill toward the Hoop Snake at the bottom.

"Do it!" I said as dust spun into the air.

Josh looked at the two Hoop snakes at the top of the hill, now beginning to roll toward us. With no better plan, Josh dropped to the ground and began rolling.

It's too bad there wasn't a camera around. Not only to document the existence of the dreaded and deadly Hoop Snake, but to also catch two grown men rolling down the hill like children.

I was about to yell, "We're gonna make it," but thought otherwise. We were coming up on the lone Hoop Snake below us. If it didn't move, we would run straight into it. Which is exactly what we did.

What happened next was a blur. The Hoop Snake at the bottom, still biting its tail and rolled into a rigid ring of terror, twitched just before we were a few feet in front of it. But at the last second it flipped its head back, straightening out and pointing its poisonous tail right at us. But because it had not been rolling at us, the spear like position it was in had no effect. It couldn't stab us or do anything other than hiss loudly. Then again, it didn't have to do much. We were the ones running into it, remember?

The good news is that I don't think the Hoop Snake was prepared for us rolling into it. The bad news was that, well, we rolled into it. But like I said, it had no way to do that much damage. We rolled right over the thing, never stopping.

It hissed even louder, and it almost seemed to moan or grunt. And I caught a good look at its face, with its eyes glowing crimson red, its black, forked tongue darting and licking the air (and nearly licking my nose), and it's sharp dagger like fangs opening up rapidly in an attempt to bite me. But it didn't. And it didn't get squished either. If it were a normal snake, it would have easily been squashed flat, but it wasn't. It felt like we rolled over a thick strip of granite rock, giving us several bruises.

"Let's go!" yelled Josh as we cleared past the Hoop Snake. He hopped up and began running.

I followed suite, race up the hill to his house. I briefly looked back (which I'm told you're never suppose to do), to see the other two Hoop Snakes stopped by the third one. Perhaps their family fun was done, already talking about "the two humans that got away."

Afterward, in the safety of Josh's house, I checked for any puncture wounds or damage. Other than a few scratches from all the rolling through the sand, rocks, and grass, we were unharmed. I did find a puncture mark in my swimsuit, right near the groin area. Apparently the Hoop Snake did in fact attack us while we rolled over it. I still have the swimsuit to prove it. But that's all we have for proof of our story. Nobody believes us of course, but that's okay. We know it's true, and I'm sure Josh's grandpa is up there in heaven somewhere, laughing at us and saying, "I told you so!"

We learned a good lesson that day. Always listen to the stories your grandpa tells you, or from anyone older, and never assume they're fake. Some, we now know, are real.

HISTORY

TWIT (TUNE WHILE I TYPE)
ALL DEAD, ALL DEAD BY QUEEN

I have to say, while fascinated with this story, I can't imagine a snake could actually bite its own tail, become rigid, and roll down a hill. And let's not forget being able to stab its prey with its pointy, venomous tail. Then again, I can't entirely disprove a Hoop Snake's existence.

The term Hoop Snake is generally accepted to have started with the Pecos Bill stories, back in the early 1900s. And most likely, Hoop Snakes fall into the same category as Pecos Bill does—being legends and folklore. Its venom is very deadly (much more dangerous than a diamondback rattler they say). It can easily kill a 200-pound man, or a 2,000-pound bull. And the only way to kill a Hoop Snake, is for it to run into its own tail.

The Hoop Snake is also mentioned in a letter from 1784 (published in *Tour, in the USA, Volume 1*). It indicates that while regular serpents crawl on their bellies, the Hoop Snake throws itself into a circle and rapidly runs after its prey.

Even though there has been no evidence to support the existence of a Hoop Snake, there have been several reports across the country, with several coming from the St. Croix River Valley area. And the naturalist, Raymond Ditmars, placed a $10,000 reward for anyone to provide evidence that the Hoop Snake in fact exists.

But the idea of a snake biting its tail goes back centuries (all the way back to Egyptian times, around 1600 B.C.). The snake back then, in Greek mythology, was called an Ouroboros, or Uroboros. Back then, the snake was said to symbolize the renewal of the universe.

This theme, of an animal biting its tail, has been seen with worms, serpents, and dragons. The symbolism can also mean infinity, perfection, and totality, or an endless round of embodied existence. My opinion, however, is that anything that bites its own tail, is either too crazy, or too hungry. Of course, I have a Golden Retriever (Sophi) at home that loves to spend half of her day chasing her tail. The other half of the day, I think her tail chases her. Perhaps dogs should be added to the Uroboros collection of animals…

Seriously, though, it's hard to imagine a snake curling up and rolling at you. But with all the history behind the creature, perhaps, in some strange way, it's true. All we need to do is spend some time searching for them in their natural habitat. Which, to the best of my knowledge, are places like the St. Croix River Valley. I haven't spent much time in that part of Minnesota; the closest I've come is Stillwater. It's a gorgeous area of the state, with crisp, clean water running from the St. Croix. And maybe that's why the Hoop Snakes are there, not to mention the sandy soil for easy burrowing (assuming a Hoop Snake needs to burrow, and doesn't live in trees—or peoples' basements).

But like any good monster story about strange creatures, you always must keep somewhat of an open mind. Maybe there are a few Hoop Snakes out there, rolling across the sands of a nearby riverbank, looking for their next meals. Might it be you? That would depend on how fast you can roll away from it. Of course, it makes more sense to have a seriously large machete in the back pocket of your swimsuit while sunning yourself on the beach. Chop Chop.

Similar to a Hoop Snake, the Ouroboros of ancient times would bite its tail as well.

WENDIGO OF ROSEAU

*"I am able to play monsters well. I understand monsters.
I understand madmen."*

- Sir Anthony Hopkins
(English Actor and Film Director. 1937-)

By all rights, I should be dead, many times over, eaten by the monsters I hunt. And one case in particular, dealing with the cannibalistic Wendigo, the chase turned tides and I was the one being hunted.

I guess you could call me an American Van Helsing, searching for monsters in the night, destroying them as to ensure they do not destroy us. Monsters, contrary to most beliefs, are real. I have seen many of them—vampires, werewolves, you name it. But there's one monster, the Wendigo, I'll never forget hunting, probably because *it* was doing the hunting, not me.

My quest to kill the Wendigo started back in the late 1880s. Yes, that's right. For me to be writing this right now in the twenty-first century, makes me the oldest man in the world. I'm well over one hundred; I guess I stopped counting many years ago. And I'm not sure why I'm still alive. I suppose that as long as there are monsters to kill, I'll be here. That is unless they get me first.

The Wendigo, which as the Native American legend goes, is ancient, having been around since before time. It shows itself from time to time, anywhere in the world, staying for several years, then leaving. Some say it sleeps in between visits, for decades, then awakens with a voracious appetite. It feeds on human flesh, yes, a cannibal. That is if we are assuming it is of human form originally. That is also debatable. Nevertheless, it is a monster by all definitions and must be stopped.

Its appearance in the small town of Roseau, Minnesota, back in the late 1800s was alarming to say the least. It started quietly, with a young girl gone missing while walking home from school one day. Then, several days later, a farmer in the fields disappeared. Within two more weeks, there were a dozen people who had vanished, leaving no trace.

Luckily, I had been nearby in the town of Milwaukee, Wisconsin, hunting down werewolves in the area, and had heard about the disappearances in Roseau, Minnesota. Nowadays, you could hop on a plane and be there in a couple hours. Back then, however, it wasn't so easy. It took me three days to get there by horse. When I got there, it was evident a monster was at play.

The folks of Roseau were panicked, terrified to come out of their homes, even during broad daylight.

"The monster – it's faster than lightning!" screamed the local man outside the general store as I interviewed him.

"A man eater!" yelled the lady from the doorway, carrying a sack of carrots and potatoes. "My son is…" she never finished her sentence, looking with tear-filled eyes out to the woods instead.

"I'm here to fix things," I said, as more gathered from the town to hear me. "I will rid this monster from your lives. It is… what I do."

Those nearby clapped, with a few cheering, hopeful that I could hold true to my promise. The trouble was, I had no idea what monster it was yet, or how to eradicate it.

I had my suspicions, though. It most likely was the Wendigo. I've heard stories about it now and then, but thought I should talk to the Shaman of the local Ojibwa Tribe, to see what he believed might be going on.

As expected, the Shaman validated my assumptions; a Wendigo was on the loose. Now I had two things to deal with. One had to do with telling the town of Roseau that they had a flesh-eating monster in the area. The other, and more important, was how to kill it. Turns out the creature doesn't like iron, steel, or silver. Iron has the least killing power, while silver was the greatest. Luckily, in my travels, I have acquired a gun that shoots silver bullets. Yes, to be used when needed for hunting werewolves. But in this case, it would be used for Wendigos.

The next step was to bring the monster out of hiding. Of course, the easiest way was to have bait. And the only thing it would want was human flesh. Being that I didn't want to alarm the folks of Roseau, I decided to keep quiet about the Wendigo, and explain to them I was hunting a giant grizzly bear. They bought into the story, and several went on the hunt with me. Although with what was about to happen, I felt horrible about lying to them. It would have been better for them to stay locked up in their homes.

The hunt began, late at night near the witching hour (the real witching hour of 3 a.m.), with torches, dogs, and rifles. It was your classic monster hunt, one I'd seen a hundred times before. What I didn't know, was how this one would end. I'd never hunted for a Wendigo; I didn't know its strengths or weaknesses very well. To make matters worse, the Wendigo knew everything about us, and used it to its advantage.

As I've indicated, in the beginning of this story, I was the one being hunted. The Wendigo knew we were out there before we were even there. It had traps setup for us, it understood our nature and could easily predict our every move. It was a natural-born hunter.

Artist's rendition of the
horrific man-eating Wendigo,
similar to ones supposedly
inhabiting northern Minnesota
and Canada.

Within minutes of setting out, the torches mysteriously blew out as a strong wind came by (no doubt the speedy Wendigo zipped through our party undetected, causing the wind). And then, one by one, the men in the group disappeared, with a scream trailing away in the distance. Before I knew it, I was alone. That is, of course, with the exception of the Wendigo, which was now standing motionless in front of me, with a tilted head as if studying me.

I'll never forget its glowing eyes floating in sunken sockets, its long, thin, blackened tongue, stabbing the air and tasting my sent, and yellow, tarnished fangs, sharpened no doubt for its current killing spree.

And it was tall, at least twice my height, but half as wide. Its skin, yellowish with shades of a shallow purple hue where veins ran dry underneath, hung draping like an old, discolored robe.

Most monsters, when confronted by me, sense the danger and ready themselves for a battle. The Wendigo on the other hand, stood tall in defiance. It was not intimidated by me. In fact, I was the one being intimidated. Never before had I dealt with such a creature, with supernatural speed, agility, and a voracious hunger for human flesh. My flesh.

As I raised my gun to shoot my silver bullets, the Wendigo cocked its head further, and I believe laughed, or snorted. At least that's what it seemed like. Then, in an instant, it was gone, just as I fired my first shot. The bullet traveled through the air, missing the Wendigo and ricocheting off an Ironwood tree.

In my years of training (with as you would expect, the great Van Helsing himself), I could sense the presence of an evil monster, not with my eyes, but with my sixth sense. I know that the Wendigo had swiftly moved behind me, only a few feet off to my left. I swung around instinctively and shot my second of three bullets.

The Wendigo, though surprised at my ability, easily shifted to the side. And while I was busy aiming for my next shot, the Wendigo was busy aiming for me. It lunged at me, its claws reaching for my chest, no doubt to rip out my heart.

Instinctively, I brought my gun to my chest. The Wendigo flinched, not wanting to touch the iron in the gun (nor the silver bullet inside). It darted at the last second to my side, rolling across the ground at lightning speed. But it didn't stay there long. Within seconds it was standing, ready to charge at me a second time.

For as much training and experience that I had acquired, none of it could have prepared me for what happened next. The Wendigo, with its brilliant hunting abilities, jumped high into the air, swiftly. It was too quick for me. By the time I had my gun ready, it was too late. The Wendigo reached at my chest with its long, needle-like claws, digging into my flesh.

I reeled at the pain, but the Wendigo missed my heart, and I was still alive. Unfortunately, my gun had fallen to the ground and I was unable to pick it up (for obvious reasons). Then, brilliance overcame me as I stared with my last breath at the nearby tree. It was Ironwood. *Could it kill the Wendigo?* It was worth a try. I ran as best I could at the tree, blood gurgling out my mouth, and impaled the Wendigo, pushing an ironwood branch through its chest and into its icy heart.

A screech, like a thousand ravens, echoed through the woods from the Wendigo as it knew it had lost. Yet, it was still alive, barely. I pulled myself from its claws, blood dripping from my wounds, and crawled to my gun. The silver bullet would finish the Wendigo off, I was sure of it. Unfortunately, as I turned to face it, gun in hand, it was gone.

Luckily, the Wendigo left the area, never to trouble the town of Roseau again. Perhaps it was intimidated by me. Or, most likely, it had filled its belly enough to sleep for another few decades. Being that rumors spread about it being back, around the 1970s in Ontario, I imagine the latter is true.

I could not find it when searching in Ontario, but perhaps I am getting too old. Perhaps it is time for a new American Van Helsing. Might you be interested? The Wendigo is due to show itself soon. But be careful, my friend, on what you wish for. Hunting monsters may be in your immediate future, like it or not.

HISTORY

TWIT (TUNE WHILE I TYPE)
THE ROOT OF ALL EVIL BY DREAM THEATER

The Wendigo (some other spellings are Windigo, Windago, and Witiko), is by far the most exciting monster reported in Minnesota, in my opinion. After all, you can't get much more terrifying than a man-eating spirit creature, whose name translates to "evil that devours," and hunts you at lightning speed in the dead of night.

Most would think the monster is the creation of Algernon Blackwood, from his short story of 1910 titled, *The Wendigo*. But the creature has been around for centuries, told through numerous Native American stories of the Algonquian cultures (such as the Ojibwa or Cree). In essence, their Wendigo was made of spirit, towering over fifteen feet tall, wearing white robes, and portrayed with a star on its forehead. And, when the monster appeared, it always meant an impending doom was to occur, involving death.

Regardless of its association with death, there are apparently those who would like to call the monster out. For what reason, I have no idea. A death wish I suppose. But, in the event you have such a calling, I've included the procedure to do so below:

Step one: Go into the forest alone, during harsh weather such as a blizzard (which would probably be your first mistake).

Step two: Strip naked and meditate, to get in touch with nature (again, another mistake in my opinion).

Step three: Recite the following words loudly –

ZIRDO - ZONG – LUCAL (I AM - OF THE WINDS - IN THE NORTH)

A - VPAAH - GIGIPAH - ZIR - UNIGLAG – CAOSG (ON - THE WINGS - OF THE LIVING BREATH - I - DESCEND - ON THE EARTH)

ZIRDO - AVAVAGO – LANSH (I AM - THE THUNDERS - IN POWER EXALTED)

BAI - LUSDAN – IALPOR (SOARING DOWN - WITH FEET – FLAMING)

NIIS - PARM - ORSBA - VEP, OBOLEN – LEVITHMONG (COME YE - RUN - DRUNKEN - AS A FLAME, YOUR GARMENTS - THE BEASTS OF THE FIELD)

ZIRDO - VRELP - DS - IALPON - SA – TRANAN (I AM - A STRONG SEETHING - THAT - BURNS - IN - THE MARROW)

IAL – GIGIPAH (CONSUME - THE ESSENCE OF LIFE)

ZAZAS ZAZAS NASATANATA ZAZAS IA WENDIGO IA WENDIGO IA WENDIGO

Then, at break neck speed, run naked through the dark forest. This will probably be the last mistake you'll ever make. Because you'll either fall off a cliff, run into a tree (or bear), or find your Wendigo. Either way, the ending doesn't sound good.

> Readers, In case you're not fully aware: I don't condone the above procedure and suggest that it is for reading enjoyment only.

There are several versions of what exactly a Wendigo is. For the most part, he is believed to be a spirit creature, once human, that takes part in cannibalistic tendencies, eating both humans as well as other Wendigos. In particular, a human can become a Wendigo if he turns to cannibalism, as would be the case if you were stranded way up north in the middle of nowhere, with no food. It is said that when a person turns to that lowly of a state of existence, the demonic Wendigo spirit enters the body, further continuing the process of cannibalism and hunger for human flesh, and is never satisfied after killing and consuming a person.

I suppose then, one important item to discuss, if you're camping in the remote regions of northern Minnesota, is what the Wendigo looks like. There are several variations, but basically the creature is skin and bones, with no muscle or fat. Its skin color can be from yellow to ash gray, with glowing, yellowish eyes sunk deep into blackened eye-sockets. The size is typically a little larger than human, or sometimes up to fifteen feet tall, but it depends on whether the creature has been feeding. The more it feeds, the larger it gets.

But it doesn't eat humans continuously (thankfully). It seems to go in spurts, where there will be sightings and disappearances in an area for several months or a few years, then nothing is reported for many years afterward. It appears to get its fill of human flesh, then hibernates for decades. Back in the 1700s there were many reports about the Wendigo in Canada, so much so that there tended to be many people on trial, accused of being a Wendigo. Canada as it were, had to deal with lots of "Wendigo Trials," similar to the situation in Salem, where there were many "Witch Trials" going on.

Basil Johnston, an Ojibwa teacher and scholar from Ontario, describes the Wendigo as such:

> The Wendigo was gaunt to the point of emaciation, its desiccated skin pulled tautly over its bones. With its bones pushing out against its skin, its complexion the ash gray of death, and its eyes pushed back deep into their sockets, the Wendigo looked like a gaunt skeleton recently disinterred from the grave. What lips it had were tattered and bloody [....] Unclean and suffering from suppurations of the flesh, the Wendigo gave off a strange and eerie odor of decay and decomposition, of death and corruption.

In the past few decades, the Wendigo has been receiving a lot of publicity, at least in horror films, competing with vampires, were-wolves, zombies, and other creatures of the night. There was a movie appropriately titled *Wendigo*, which portrayed one of the creatures. Other movies include *Ravenous*, or *Frostbiter: Wrath of the Wendigo*. There have also been several television shows portraying the Wendigo, such as *Charmed*, *Supernatural*, and *Blood Ties*. And let's not forget video games: *Final Fantasy*, *Hexen*, *Warcraft Universe*, and the classic *Dungeons & Dragons*. Even the Digimon world has a Wendigo, which is called Wendigomon.

Even books such as Stephen King's *Pet Sematary*, has references to a Wendigo (which had "soured the land in the cemetery, making everything come to life that was buried there"). Wendigos are also in comic books, in particular Marvel Comics Universe.

The Wendigo phenomena has even entered the scientific community, with a certain psychosis named after it (officially spelt Windigo Psychosis). It is a mental disorder involving one having an insatiable appetite for human flesh, combined with a fear of becoming a cannibal. Of course, I'm thinking if you already have the first symptom, you don't have to worry too much about the second one.

One of the more notable Windigo Psychosis cases is from a Plains Cree fur trapper in Alberta Canada, back in 1878. His name was Swift Runner (which may have helped when trapping bears). During one winter, he and his family were short of food, with his eldest son eventually dying. Swift Runner turned to cannibalism shortly thereafter, and continued to feast and kill the rest of his family. He was eventually captured, confessed his addiction to human flesh, and was executed at Fort Saskatchewan.

The other famous case of Windigo Psychosis involved Jack Fiddler, an Ojibwa chief and shaman from the early 1900s in Canada. He apparently had special powers, or magic, able to defeat Wendigos— sort of an American Van Helsing monster hunter. With his brother, Joseph, the two of them would hunt down those supposedly afflicted with Windigo Psychosis (or other monster illnesses), and euthanize them. Canadian authorities eventually captured Jack, who later committed suicide. But his brother, Joseph, was executed.

Whether the Wendigo is psychological, physical, or spiritual, the end result of cannibalism isn't good. One option, however, to prevent the situation from occurring, is to perform a Native American ceremonial dance. The last known dance (known as wiindigookaanzhimow) was done at Leech Lake Indian Reservation in northern Minnesota by the Ojibwa tribe. No report on how the dance went, but since there's no new reports of Wendigos in Minnesota, perhaps it worked. Just like why I carry an elephant gun around, to fend off any elephants (it works, right?).

The last known sighting of a Wendigo was in 1997, up in Ontario, Canada by an American trucker near St. Catherine's as he was passing through the town. So it seems the creature has not entirely disappeared. It may show up in our neck of the woods, perhaps on your next campout. And it will wait patiently for those that stray too far from the trail, or take that midnight nature hike. You may hear its shrieking in the night and panic. But don't worry – it's just a Wendigo, hungry for your flesh.

Fieldtrip

While putting together this book, determining which monsters should be included and which shouldn't, it was obvious that the Wendigo needed to be here. Furthermore, I looked into which monsters I should attempt to investigate myself. Again, Wendigos in Roseau was at the top of the list. Why? Well, to me, it's the most exciting. And of course, it was also the most dangerous. After all, running through the woods late at night in northern Minnesota on the edge of nothing but forest can't be all that smart to do. What's worse, is that I did it by myself.

There are certain rules you try to follow as a monster hunter (see the chapter on monster hunting in this book); seeking creatures of the night by yourself is most certainly a bad idea. Even camping alone, especially in bear country, is not too smart. Still, it's doable if you take the right precautions, which of course I did not.

So with no friends willing to hunt with me (cluck cluck, Mr. Chickens), and a healthy supply of Monster energy drinks, I ventured into the northern Minnesota nothingness of green towering trees and shrubbery at Hayes Lake State Park, just outside of Roseau. I thought to myself, this is perfect—for the Wendigo that is. I'm excellent bait. A man, camping alone, searching through the dark forest at night. I was sure that the spirit of Wendigo was thrilled, drooling at its easy catch.

To make matters worse, I didn't get to my campsite until ten minutes before dark. I don't know about you, but I'm not too keen on pitching tents in the dark—especially with Wendigos lurking in the distance. With seconds to spare, as the dotted shadows of the surrounding trees turned into one thick blanket of darkness, I sat in my camp chair (with the tent up and a fire built), waiting for the creatures to appear.

Okay, so I wasn't completely alone. There were two other campers in the area, although they were in motor-homes. I'm thinking that if a Wendigo did show up, it will surely try my tent first. Not good. It's like they say about burglars—you lock your door at night to make the burglar go to the next house that's not locked. My tent, with its flimsy nylon walls, gave me little comfort that a Wendigo would not come knocking.

I started a fire, providing some warmth from the chilling late September night. It also gave me some comfort from the blackness dancing just out of reach. But I knew this was not where I could stay. After all, I was hunting monsters, right? Or were they hunting me? Thoughts turned to the wild hunter skills of the Wendigo, how it could easily stalk you, capturing you as its simple prey. I briefly thought of jumping in my car and heading home, but quickly reminded myself that I was over eight hours away from Rochester, and did not want to come back up again.

So I mounted my trail camera on a nearby tree, ready to take pictures of my campsite, and of course pictures of the Wendigo as it tried to eat me in the middle of the night. Next, I grabbed my digital audio recorder (named D.A.R.R.E.N. for Digital Audio Recorder of Really Eerie Noises, from my ghost hunting days, written about in my other freakish book, *Ghosts of Southeastern Minnesota*) and did some E.V.P. (Electronic Voice Phenomena) work. I figured, if the Wendigo is from a spirit, it may be able to talk to me through my digital audio recorder. Then I'd have a recording of it, to prove to the rest of the world that they exist. That is, if I survived.

Next, I put fresh batteries in my night-vision camcorder and, you guessed it, headed out into the forest. No, I repeat, no, I did not strip and go naked, as prescribed earlier in the history section. I figured it would be hard enough to explain to the park ranger why I was out in the middle of the night with a camera; running around naked would have made things much worse. I did, however, recite some of the incantations that supposedly bring the Wendigo to you.

I wandered through the woods, all the while my camcorder recording, with me wondering two things; one, what do I do if a Wendigo shows up? And two, what in the world was I doing out here in the first place? I mean, let's get real. I'm a writing kind of guy, not a monster hunter. Furthermore, I didn't have much of a plan for if a bear came at me (other than the small can of pepper spray I had). Thankfully, there were no major incidents, and I eventually returned to camp, tired and exhausted and ready for some sleep.

And it should be obvious, I didn't run into any Wendigos, being that I'm still writing this book (no, it doesn't end similar to Monty Python's *Holy Grail* with the Black Beast of Arrrggghhh). I did, however, find something interesting while reviewing the audio, video, and trail camera pictures. The trail camera caught what appears to be a phantom, ghostly figure by my fire, after it had mostly gone out. It looks like some thin, spindly, creature squatting low by the fire, peering into it. It startled me at first, but then I thought it might be wisps of smoke from the low burning embers. Or, just maybe, it was the spirit of the Wendigo, inspecting my fire shortly after I retired.

Photo of an evil spirit creature, kneeling
near the fire pit outside author's tent while
hunting Wendigos in northern Minnesota
near Canada. Could this be the spirit form
of a Wendigo?

Outline of
Wendigo as seen
by the author in
photo above.

The rest of the night was uneventful, other than a few peculiar sounds I heard deep into the forest somewhere. Being that I was paranoid about a Wendigo crashing through my tent, or perhaps a bear, I didn't get much sleep. Still, I have to say the event was amazingly peaceful. I was surprised to find out how relaxing it was, sitting at the edge of the wilderness alone at a crackly campfire with nothing but the trees and brightly twinkling stars above. Quite rewarding if you ask me. Or maybe I was in shock, dumbfounded at my stupidity in hunting monsters alone. Either way, I considered the fieldtrip a success—I didn't find a Wendigo, but perhaps I found myself.

WHITEFACE ICEMAN

"I beheld the wretch – the miserable monster whom I had created."

– Mary Wollstonecraft Shelley
(English Novelist of Frankenstein 1797-1851)

The nightmare continues. Every day I still see the image of a large, hairy, ape-like creature coming at me through the woods north of Duluth, with hunger in its eyes – hunger for me.

I am the creator of the Iceman. You may have heard of it. It was very big back in the late 60s. A carnival show of sorts, costing only two bits. But the truth to this creature is priceless; and I think it is time for all to know.

The Iceman is real.

To this day, I'm not entirely sure what kind of creature it was, but definitely not human. There are many stories as to its origin, but only I know the real truth. It all started back in the early 1960s, on a hunting trip for deer, just north of Duluth. I was a pretty good hunter, having done many trips before. And having served this great country in the armed forces, I was a sharp shooter as well. But this time, my hunting skills and commando experiences were tested beyond belief.

With the sun not yet up, my two friends and I left the comfort of our cabin off the gently rolling shores of the nearly frozen Whiteface Reservoir. Loons called in the distance, sending echoes into the forest, signaling that we were far from civilization. A chilling fog slowly pushed across what little open water there was, spilling over onto the crisp, frosty, dew-sprinkled shoreline. It was just ourselves and the deer, or so we thought.

It didn't take long for us to spot a few doe rummaging around on the forest floor. We didn't have any deer stands to use, but found an excellent ridge to rest in, waiting for the prey to appear. We passed on some smaller does, wanting something much larger. As for myself, I was hoping for a large buck, at least 8 points. I had no desire to be called a Bambi killer, the animal I would bring down had to be worthy of the task. And I couldn't have been closer to the truth.

"There she is!" yelled my partner, his frozen breath rolling into the air. He also had armed forces experience. We peered into the distance, spotting a large doe grazing on the nearby grass. Luckily the wind was blowing toward us, not allowing the deer to sense our presence easily.

A sketch of the Iceman, as it lay in its frozen slab of ice for viewing at State Fairs across the country around the 1970s.

Bam! Bam! Ba-bam! Before I could say anything, my friends had blasted away at the unsuspecting doe, causing it to falter a moment, then scurry away. Luckily, they were a lousy shot.

"What ya shooting at?" I asked, upset they shot so blindly.

"A big doe," they nodded. "Huge."

I shook my head. "Yeah, right." Looking into the distance, I could tell it was gone. "Well, it's probably miles away by now."

To be sure, we climbed down to the location and investigated. To our surprise, we found blood on the shrubs nearby. "Must of grazed it," I said, still not convinced it was a clean hit.

My friend disagreed. "No, there's a lot of blood here." He looked into the forest, squinting at the afternoon sunlight piercing through the canopy of leaves overhead. He pointed and added, "Probably should track it down."

Well, I had no desire to track down a deer with a slight flesh wound. It would probably take all weekend, and even then we'd have to shoot it again. Still, hunting was a sport, and this was a great challenge. I agreed to search for the semi-fallen doe, while the others traveled further into the forest and continued hunting.

As suspected, I searched for hours. What a waste. But the challenge of trying to find the hurt animal was exciting, to say the least. I was able to track the blood stained leaves deep into the forest, far into areas of northern Minnesota where most people don't go. Several times I stopped, catching my bearings, and wondering what I was doing. Especially when the forest turned into more of a frozen swamp than anything.

But I kept searching. At this point, nearly lost, the quest was more for my own satisfaction of testing my hunting skills, rather than the actual venison. Besides, there was no way for me to drag the deer out of the swamp. There wasn't a road for miles.

Just as I was going to give up, being that it was late in the day (the sun was nearly setting), I heard a strange gurgling sound in the distance. I moved the branches in front of me away, crouching low, and nearly screamed.

Three strange and totally hairy creatures were leaning over my fallen dear, gorging themselves on its blood and flesh.

I stared, motionless with fear, wondering what to do next. I didn't have to do anything. One of the three monsters saw me, while turning to feast on a leg, and howled this high-pitched scream that sent chills deep into my bones.

What happened next was confusing to say the least. One of the hairy creatures charged at me. I was still having trouble trying to figure out if it was a bear, or something else. With it running at me on two legs, flapping its arms high in the air, I was sure it was no bear.

Instinct, thankfully, took over, with me firing a shell at the beast. With it only a few feet from me, my shot hit him directly in the eye, sending the creature twirling forward, on top of me. I screamed briefly, horrified by the incident, before collecting myself and pushing the monster off me and on to the frozen ground.

The other two creatures, most likely just as frightened as I was, ran away. As for myself, I did that very same thing, in the opposite direction. I pushed myself through the lightly frozen swamps, crashing into bushes and banging off of trees, until I was a couple miles away.

After firing three shots into the air (a sign of distress), a nearby hunting party found me. I explained that I was lost, not wanting to go into any details about the horrific monsters I ran into. I just wanted to get out of there. Alive. Who knows, the other creatures might have been following me, waiting for their moment to jump and eat me alive.

Luckily, nothing like that happened. Instead, I was the one hungry – hungry for the truth. *What did I shoot out there in the wilderness? Was it a large gorilla? Or maybe just a bear?* I had to find out.

Weeks later, I got up enough nerve to go back. It wasn't easy, but I had to know for sure if I was a murderer, worried it may have been some guy dressed in a hairy, monkey costume. Or maybe I had killed some unknown creature. I was hoping, of course, that perhaps I dreamed the whole thing up.

Unfortunately, my hopes were shattered as I stood hours later in the frosty marsh over the frozen bloodied creature.

It certainly didn't look human, but it definitely wasn't an ape – much too tall and large for that. I studied the creature closer, my frosty breath trailing into the air, looking over my shoulder at every sound nearby, wondering if its friends would come back at any moment. I was prepared, though, with my shotgun close by. If I could shoot one of the monsters, I could shoot more, right?

Thankfully, I didn't have to worry about that. No other monsters showed up while I stood there gawking at the frozen corpse. But the next question was, what do I do with the body? What if someone else found it, shot dead with a bullet through its eye? After thinking for awhile, with a fresh dusting of snow beginning to fall, I decided it was best to get rid of all evidence—including the creature itself.

To make a long story short, I spent the entire day (and much of the night) removing the body, picking and chopping away at the marshy ice surrounding it. I hauled it away in my swamp buggy, loading it into my pickup truck, destined for home. Then the only concern I had was where to store it. Oh, and what I would tell my wife.

Of the two, telling my wife was the easiest. It seems she was happy to know I was out with some strange monster, rather than in the bars with strange women. But storing the creature, well, that was another problem altogether.

What we finally concluded on doing was to throw it in the freezer we had in the basement. And, after many hours of freezing, the creature was hidden, away from others and authorities. After all, I still wasn't clear on whether I'd committed a crime or not. Or if I had the find of the century—the missing link between man and beast.

One thing led to another, and it was years before I decided it was time to showcase my neanderthalic find. After much research, I was fairly comfortable I had done nothing wrong. So, to celebrate my findings, I shared it with all who wanted to see it. For a price of course—two bits to be exact. My Iceman as it came to be called, toured the Midwest for several years, on display at many fairs, only outdone by the occasional bearded lady or sword-swallowing dwarf.

This story could end at this moment, with my frozen monster eternally remembered on a global scale as the piece of the puzzle between man and Neanderthal, discovered finally by scientist and my name goes down in history as "the guy that shot the missing link." But that's not how this ends. Sure, I did invite two gentlemen from the scientific community to analyze my monster, and they did in fact become astounded by it. So much so that they published their findings in science journals, validating my creature as authentic.

Unfortunately, the new found publicity caught the eye of local authorities, including the FBI. At this point, I did not want to take any chances of being called a murderer, being put away behind bars for the rest of my life. So I concocted a replica of the monster, to use on my tours. And what did I do with the real monster? Well, that's how this story truly ends.

My original plan was to bury the monster, somewhere nobody could find it. Or maybe even burn the thing. Either way, I'd give it a proper burial, sending it off to monster heaven I suppose. But I didn't have to.

The monster's friends, after all this time, finally showed up.

Yes, in the middle of the night, like aliens at the foot of your bed, two large, hairy ape-like creatures grunted and snorted at me, with their glowing yellow eyes staring back at me.

It didn't take long for me to figure out what they wanted. For some reason I had been expecting them for quite some time; initially they visited in my dreams. But now, they were here, in the flesh. They kept pointing to the floor, down below where their friend was kept in the freezer.

I can't blame them for their actions. If I were kept frozen for several years, I'd want to be laid to rest, or whatever their plans were for their fallen comrade. Without thinking, I got up and led them to the basement. A few times I thought about grabbing my shotgun and blowing them away, but then I thought about how tired I was of this whole mess. It was time to get rid of it, time to move on, and time to put things to rest. Literally.

With not much effort, the hairy creatures ripped apart my freezer, freeing their friend from its chilly confines. The two of them lifted their comrade with little effort, up the creaking stairs and out the side door, never to be seen again.

The years have passed since then, and I now have no proof to my story, which is just as good. A mystery such as this perhaps is best remaining a mystery. You see, I feel sorry for the creatures I discovered, and am glad they are back in the wilderness, with us left wondering once again if they are real. I know they are real, and that's good enough for me.

HISTORY

TWIT (TUNE WHILE I TYPE)
HELL'S BELLS BY AC/DC

The Minnesota Iceman is by far one of the most famous monster stories from Minnesota, occurring back in the mid 1960s. As the above story indicates, Frank Hansen, a retired Air Force Captain and pilot, apparently found himself face-to-face with the tall, hairy creature while out deer hunting near the Whiteface Reservoir in northern Minnesota (over 50 miles from Duluth).

Hansen had separated from his hunting party, tracking down a deer he had shot. After a mile or two of trudging through the cold, frosty swamps, he found his deer. Only that's not all he found. Three hairy creatures were standing over his deer, tearing into it, making gurgling sounds as they gorged themselves on the fresh kill. One of the creatures eventually noticed Hansen, and began running and screeching toward him. Hansen instinctively raised his rifle and shot, hitting it in the eye.

Startled, Hansen ran away, never really sure what had happened. After finally meeting up with the other hunters in the group, he decided not to tell anyone about what he'd saw. But as the weeks went by, he was puzzled by what he'd experienced. He concluded that something strange had happened, and that he had to go back.

He returned to the scene, the first week of December, with a fresh layer of snow covering the area. He brought along an ATV 4-wheeler, to carry the body back and give it a proper burial. He eventually found the creature, frozen and bloody, and shot in the eye, just like Hansen remembered. But the corpse was frozen into the ground, and he needed tools to remove it. So he went back home, coming back later with a pick, a shovel, and a chainsaw.

With the creature loaded up into his truck, he headed back home to Duluth. But there was one flaw in his plan; the ground was too frozen to give the creature a proper burial. So, for unknown reasons, Hansen decided to put the creature in his new freezer (after much convincing and discussion with his wife) down in the basement. The corpse was

now thawing out, and stinking—all the more reason to get it frozen once again.

The plan was to bury the corpse in the spring, and continued to keep it in his freezer. They poured water into the freezer, encapsulating the cadaver in a thick block of ice. And as spring approached, Hansen tried to figure out how to thaw the creature out and bury it. But the months passed, and Hansen and his wife decided to move to Rollingstone Minnesota (due to his recent retirement), transporting the frozen creature with them. Of course, moving a monster corpse would not be easy, especially with a moving company. Hansen decided to keep the corpse in the freezer, locking it up, and having friends help move it.

Months passed, with the monster still frozen in his basement, and Hansen continued to think about what to do with the strange creature. He concluded that it was not human (thankfully), but that it was some as of yet undiscovered beast—half-man, half-ape perhaps. And, as one thing led to another, Hansen began to think the creature should be put on display, for all to see. After all, who wouldn't want to get a glimpse of a prehistoric man, possible the missing link?

He decided the monster could be displayed at various carnivals across the Midwest. But the problem was with transporting a real cadaver. There were laws in some cases about doing this, not to mention the danger in having it unthaw. In the end, Hansen decided to create a replica of the creature, displaying that instead.

By 1967, with the help of some Hollywood makeup artists (including Bud Westmore of Universal, and Howard Ball of the Los Angeles County Museum), a fake model of the strange monsters was created, ready for a tour.

The debut of the fake creature was on May 3rd, 1967, labeled as a "What is it?" attraction. And instead of explaining that he killed it on a hunting expedition north of Duluth, he said it was discovered frozen, floating in the Bering Straits by Japanese fishermen. The show was a success, but most experts agreed that the creature was a fake. This, of course, made Hansen decide to bring the real creature on tour next year.

Showing the real monster was a huge success. But now scientists, college students, and doctors were showing up. And the publicity was getting out of hand. And by December 1968, Terry Cullen, a college student in Chicago, ended up contacting Ivan T. Sanderson, a famous naturalist and author of strange creatures like the abominable snowmen.

Sanderson, along with Dr. Bernard Heuvelmans, a respected cryptozoologist, visited the strange monster Hansen had on display. They asked Hansen if they could inspect it further. Hansen reluctantly agreed, worried they may publish a scientific report on the find. And that, of course, is exactly what they ended up doing.

After several days of investigating the creature, Sanderson and Heuvelmans concluded it was authentic, based on the stench, plant matter on its teeth, and lice on its skin. In 1969, they published a report in the Royal Institute of Natural Sciences of Belgium, stating that it was an "ape-man" or "missing link." Between the report, and Sanderson mentioning the Iceman on the Tonight Show, news about the creature spread across the country. Even the Smithsonian was interested in finding out more about the strange creature.

Speculation began to develop, on how the creature was shot, and if it was a crime. This was something Hansen did not want to deal with. But he had no choice. In the end, the strange monster dubbed the Iceman, mysteriously disappeared, hidden "away from the Midwest."

The fake monster, however, continued to be displayed. And everyone began to believe there never was a real cadaver, yet those who had seen the actual corpse, swear to this day that it was the real deal. And photos taken of the exhibit during the time it was the real monster, and when it was fake, clearly show differences between them.

While the Iceman was a hot topic back in the 1960s, it's still brought up from time to time, and those having seen the monster on display, wonder if what they saw was real, or a hoax. Of course, without a real body, it's impossible to say. Most would agree that this would be a fake, carnival attraction, just to make a few bucks. But at only 25 cents per viewing (50 cents in later years), it's doubtful Hansen got very rich.

To this day, the real body of the monster has never been found. Hansen was, back in 1970, willing to give up the corpse, provided he get amnesty for any criminal or legal issues. He apparently never received any agreement, and the monster's ice-covered cadaver was never seen again.

The fake body, however, went through state fairs for several more years, into the late 1970s. I faintly recall seeing it from a distance, back in the mid 1970s at the Minnesota State Fair, but was too young to see it up close, being that I was only eight or nine at the time. And Frank Hansen has also apparently disappeared. The last reported interview with Hansen was in 1995, where he still wasn't sure what the creature was.

As to whether the Iceman is real or a hoax, well, that will probably always remain a mystery. Unless Mr. Hanson has some confessions to make on his deathbed, if in fact he's still alive. But I have to say, I have different thoughts now, every time I open the freezer at home. I just hope there's no iceman buried at the bottom.

WIZARDS OF ANGLE INLET

"Do not meddle in the affairs of Wizards, for they are subtle and quick to anger."

- Gandalf
from J.R.R. Tolkien's *The Lord of the Rings*

Do you believe in witches, warlocks and wizards? I never did, until I met one.

Actually, I met three of them. Up in Angle Inlet, northern Minnesota in the Lake of the Woods area. I had a fishing trip with some buddies of mine that I'll never forget.

I'd driven all day from Esther, Iowa, to meet some friends for fishing up in northern Minnesota, Angle Inlet. After hundreds of miles, well after midnight, my 1965 GMC pickup truck was acting up. A loud knocking developed from underneath the hood, and my rusty-but-trusty vehicle was no more.

For those of you who have never visited the Great Northwest, let me tell you, it can be a place of both splendor and fright. During the day, while the sun's peaking above the forest canopy, a feeling of beauty can overwhelm you as birds chirp cheerful melodies in the distance. But in the nighttime, well, it can be a scary ordeal to say the least.

Northern Minnesota, is a wilderness, with an emphasis on "wild." Large bears, moose, and other creatures wander quietly through the forest during the day, but at night, they thrive. So the last thing I wanted to do, was to be stranded in the middle of nowhere, among the creatures of the night.

Armed only with a small flashlight with rusty, corroding batteries, and a gun with even rustier bullets, being that I hadn't used it for several years, I had no choice but to hoof it to the nearest town, which was miles away. I'd been up in this area many times before for fishing trips, and knew there wouldn't be a car traveling by for possibly hours, especially this late at night. No, the only thing I'd probably run into was something furry with a hungry growl.

As I started my lonely walk down the dark, moonlit road, I noticed a faint glow coming from somewhere deep within the woods. I initially thought it might be a cabin, or perhaps a camper with a campfire. Either way, it would be a welcome sight, much better than meeting a bear or moose further down the road.

I decided to hike into the woods toward the light. It seemed to be only a few hundred yards away, but as I kept walking, it never got closer. It felt like hours had passed and I'd still not made it to the light. Then, when I was about to give up, the light was only a few yards away. Excited to have finally made it, I jumped into the small clearing where the light was emanating from.

I have to admit, I was a little scared. Being out in the forest, miles from any civilization, the light could be anything. But at this point I didn't have many options. I had probably wandered into the forest for several miles, and would no doubt have a terrible time trying to find my way out, at least during the night.

A drawing of a wizard, perhaps time traveling from a different era, and similar to the ones found in northern Minnesota (although perhaps not quite as large).

But I was safe, right? I had a flashlight and a gun – what else did I need? Well, for one thing, a pair of glasses might have helped. Because what I saw didn't make any sense. My heart pounded fiercely as I watched the light, now a glowing yellow orb about the size of a beach ball, pulsate and hum at me. What was even more strange, was that there were three figures standing near it.

And it wasn't like they were there all relaxed, roasting marshmallows. They were stiff, in a rigid, tightfisted stance, mesmerized by the glowing ball of light.

While I was fearful for my life, shaking uncontrollably (and dropping my gun for that matter), I called out to them. "Hey!" Looking back on this, I wondered why I was that stupid to yell. I mean, they could have been mass murderers, or crazy drug smugglers. But it was like I was forced into yelling. Weird indeed.

But just as I was getting used to the crazy scene, it changed. Right before my eyes, the three shadowy figures transformed into clearer images, human form, but dressed in weird clothing. And the large, glowing light, turned into a regular flickering and crackling campfire.

I approached them closer, now able to see their strange clothes better. I turned to my gun, which was still on the ground, thinking about picking it up.

"Need not do you?" said one of the men, who wore a cape.

His English was strange, to say the least. But his cape – that was even weirder. And he wore a thick, purple, pullover shirt, with matching purple tweed pants. And his boots were made of dark brown leather, and ran tall, almost to his knees.

The second man wore short, blue pants that looked like knickers, and a dark, black sweater tucked into his pants. And his shoes were tan colored, thin, and short with no laces. His head was bald, clean shaven, front to back.

The third and final man was wearing a long, grayish-colored cloak that hung to his ankles, with purple pants, a thick, yellow shirt, and high leather boots. He had long, brown hair that reached beyond his shoulders, and he had a thick, bushy mustache with matching eyebrows.

From what I could tell, they didn't have any cars, or camping equipment, or food. It was just themselves and the weird, twinkling fire.

As I had said, I yelled to them, startling them initially. They stared at me, like I was some kind of freak, intruding on their fun. I, on the other hand, was confident they were the freaks. But within seconds, their strange looks subsided, and they began to act normal. Well, they *tried* to act usual. But it was obvious they were not locals.

"Hey," I said again, and began to talk about my dead pickup truck. But they didn't seem to be listening.

Finally, after a long and awkward silence, the bald guy said in a broken English, "You have lathed your feet and joined us here to be happy! All three!"

I took a step back, confused at what he said. This guy was obviously crazy. Or maybe a foreigner, like from Russia or Romania. I had heard about illegal immigrants sneaking to the United States through Canada. Perhaps this was one such case.

The guy with the cape came toward me, pushing the bald man away. Then he asked, "The Aeon? Is it of Sir?"

"I'm sorry," I replied. "I'm not sure what you mean. What's an Aeon?"

The three strangers looked at each other, as if perhaps reading each other's mind. Finally, the caped man said, "You more to say. We hear more to say!"

Man, these guys were weird indeed. They were certainly either drug smugglers, or from a foreign country. It was difficult to understand what they were saying. But also, I began to wonder if this was something more. The air around me felt energized, electrified with strange power that left the hair on the back of my neck standing.

I tried talking with them more, but it was just too awkward. While they seemed nice enough, I had the feeling they were from another world, or maybe another time. And if that was the case, I needed to get out of there before things got even weirder.

As I waved goodbye to them, backing out of there slowly, the man in the cape smiled and said, "For positive, yes!"

The walk back to the road only took a few minutes, much faster than the trip into the woods. And I'm not sure how I was able to find the road in the dead of night. But I wasn't going to complain.

I walked for about two hours, covering around ten miles, all the while thinking about the three strange men. Which was fine by me – much better than thinking about the bears and moose no doubt roaming around and looking for their next meal. Especially since I had forgotten my gun.

I eventually made it to the cabin in Angle Inlet, just as the sun poked above the morning horizon. My buddies teased me to no end, after telling them about the three strange men. Which was the same reaction I get every time I bring it up to others. I try not to talk about it, but it's hard to keep it out of my head, even when it happened years ago.

I did some research on the word they said, "Aeon." Turns out it's a form of the word, "eon," meaning a long period of time. I then began to wonder if perhaps the three mean were in fact time travelers. Wizards perhaps. If only I had the guts at the time to stay there. The questions I could have asked—and the answers I would have received.

I still travel to northern Minnesota to go fishing with my friends. But I have a new GMC truck, along with a powerful flashlight, and an even more powerful gun. And I keep an eye out for lights in the forest, hoping it may be my wizard friends again, maybe willing to take me on a ride through time that I will never forget.

HISTORY

TWIT (TUNE WHILE I TYPE)
PINBALL WIZARD BY THE WHO

When I first saw this story, I began to wonder about what else could be living up in northern Minnesota, in the tip of the state. In the winter, near International Falls (known as the Icebox of the Nation), I could imagine penguins and polar bears, with it getting so cold. But wizards? That seemed highly doubtful.

But as the story goes, from a man living in Esther, Iowa, there's wizards up there. He apparently ran into them back in August of 1991, on his way to Northwest Angle Resort after his pick-up truck died on him. With nowhere to go, he began walking down the road to the next town. He saw lights flickering in the forest, so decided to go there, thinking it was a cabin or campfire. But it wasn't.

He noticed a large glowing globe on the ground, with three men standing around it. But the men were "stiff and strange," dressed in odd clothes and wearing capes. Then, as the three men noticed the young man, the glowing globe changed into a regular campfire. The three men began talking to the stranded man, but they were difficult to understand, talking in gibberish for the most part.

The young man stepped closer to the three men and waved hello. The three men tried to smile, and one of them said, "You have lathed your feet and joined us here to be happy! All three!" The young man couldn't understand what they were saying. It was like they were using the wrong words, or randomly picking them out of a dictionary.

What was stranger, reported the young man, was that the three strange looking men didn't have any camping equipment—no tents, food, or sleeping bags. And there was no car, or any tools to make a fire with. And after talking with them awhile longer, and still not able to understand them, the young man decided it was time to leave. He found the road again, and walked over ten miles to Angle Inlet.

Weeks later, the young man was still puzzled as to who he'd encountered. He wasn't sure if they were time travelers, wizards of another era perhaps. Regardless, it was a strange situation to say the least.

I found it interesting that there are many people that believe wizards exist. Perhaps not like the ones in Harry Potter's world (sorry Dumbledore), but there are those men who practice magic. Women who practice magic, on the other hand, are called witches. And there are those who claim to be witches, who practice Wicca (a religion heavily involved with nature and the elements around us). So, there may in fact be wizards and witches out there, but do they perform magic? If they are, it's not too obvious. Then again, if I could perform magic, real magic, would I be telling anyone? I'm thinking it might ruin the fun.

So to me, the likelihood of wizards practicing magic in the remote parts of northern Minnesota is next to nothing. But then again, Bigfoot shouldn't exist either. Or Pepie the Lake Monster. But these monsters and others are reported frequently. So perhaps, like any good monster hunter, you drive out there and check it out. Who knows, maybe you'll run into Dumbledore—but hopefully not Voldemort.

Drawing of an evil looking troll that is
supposedly lurking around Minnesota.

NOW DO YOU BELIEVE IN MONSTERS?

"The piano is a monster that screams when you touch its teeth."

– Andre Segovia
(Spanish classical guitarist 1893 – 1987)

No Minnesota book about monsters can conclude without a monstrous (albeit humorous) Sven and Ole story:

It was October, in the small town of Nimrod, which is south of Park Rapids, not to be confused with Grand Rapids. Sven, an avid fisherman (an angling legend in his own mind), was reading the local newspaper, becoming curious about an article on a local lake monster. It seems there was a sighting in a lake farther north of Nimrod, Lake Winnibigoshish. Sven, in his infinite wisdom, decided he should catch the monster, being the avid and legendary fisherman he was.

But he would need help. There was only one man alive that could assist Sven, and that was Ole. The only trouble would be convincing Ole's wife, Lena, to let Ole go on a fishing trip to catch a lake monster.

"Ole?" asked Sven from his rotary dial phone. "Dis is Sven."

"Sven?" responded Ole. There was a slight pause. "Oh, dat Sven. How da heck are ya?"

"Good enough. But I got dis favor ta ask ya."

"Ya?" said Ole, but then there was a click.

"Who's dat on da phone Ole?" came a low grumbling female voice. Without hesitation, she added, "Is dat you Sven?" A quick hrumph and a sigh. "We don't want yer kind here." She then hung up the phone, thinking it would hang up Ole's phone too. But it didn't.

"You still der?" whispered Sven.

"Yep," whispered Ole.

"You want ta hunt a lake monster?"

Ole thought for a moment, then asked, "Where? In da bathtub?"

"Nope. Up at dat der lake Winnibigoshishoshish."

Another slight pause, then noises were heard, screams and bantering, most likely from Lena as she caught Ole still on the phone. Then the phone went dead.

After a moment, Sven hung up, but just as he did, the phone rang.

"You still der Sven?" came the voice on the other end. It was Ole.

"Ya. You betchya."

"When do we go?" asked Ole. "I like dis monster hunt. But what does a lake monster look like?"

"Beats me," said Sven with a beaming smile. "But der's only one way ta find out."

Sven didn't ask Ole how he convinced Lena he could go; Sven didn't want to know. Being the bachelor that Sven was, he didn't have to answer to anyone. He felt sorry for Ole, then again, he felt more sorry for Lena, knowing how absent-minded Ole could be.

"Ya mean ta tell me ya furgot yer fishing pole?" said Sven to Ole, shaking his head, as they stood on the shores of Lake Winnibigoshish. "How we supposed ta catch da lake monster?"

"I brought da bait," said Ole, holding up his lunchbox. He opened it up, revealing three large chunks of cheese; one Limburger, one Havarti, and the last was a thick slice of Jarlsberg. "We'll see which one is da best."

"Ya, but first we need a boat," said Sven.

They walked to a local marina, and with luck were able to rent a nice 16 foot fishing boat (but only after throwing in a small slice of Jarlsberg). But as they set out on the water, they quickly realized there was no motor.

"Guess we'll just have ta push it," said Ole.

Sven rolled his eyes and shook his head, while looking to the sky. "Ole, we can't just jump out and push!" Sven began to undress to his undergarments. "We'll have to swim!"

So Sven and Ole took turns swimming and pushing the boat out across the lake, with the other one using an oar to steer.

Finally, Sven commanded, "Dis is da place!"

"What?" asked Ole, who was busy treading water.

"Dis is where da lake monster is!"

"How do ya know?"

He put his hand in the water, then raised a finger to the wind. "It just is. I can feel it in my bones."

"Works fer me," said Ole, who was mighty tired of pushing and swimming the boat across the lake. He jumped back in, then asked, "So how do ya catch da lake monster?"

"With da cheese," replied Sven, "and our bare hands." Sven proceeded to grab a chunk of Limburger, squishing it in his hand, then thrusting his arm into the water, swirling it around like a meandering fish.

Ole, in his own infinite wisdom, grabbed the Havarti and did the same thing. But he did so from the same side of the boat, which ended up tossing the two of them into the water, and losing their Limburger and Havarti cheese bait.

"Now what do we do?" asked Ole.

"We still got da Jarlsberg," replied Sven. So he reached into the boat and grabbed the Jarlsberg cheese. He split it into two pieces, with each of them floating in the water, swirling the cheese around.

It didn't take long for the lake monster to appear.

"Dat's it!" yelled Sven. "Da lake monster!"

Three ripples emerged from the calm lake, about ten yards apart, with the first one noticeably larger than the others. The front ripple then rose from the lake's horizon, until you could clearly see it was the head of the beast, with glowing red eyes and sharp dagger-like fangs. A spiky tail flicked and splashed about 40 yards away. It was coming toward them, sniffing the air for the Jarlsberg cheese.

"Grab it when it gets close!" whispered Sven from the water. "We'll throw it in da boat."

Ole, who was not the sharpest tool in the local Ace Hardware store, nodded in agreement, although the look on his face told you he wasn't entirely sure about it fitting in the boat.

As the lake monster lunged for the cheese in Ole's hand, Ole jumped on the beast. Sven threw his cheese at the monster and yelled, "Get him!" before hopping on top of the slippery beast as well.

For a few brief seconds, there was an amazing sight to see. Two men and a lake monster, wrapped around each other, one struggling for the cheese, the other two just simply struggling. And in a few seconds more, it was over, with the lake's surface returning to its pristine mirrored shine.

Sven and Ole hung with one arm from the side of their rented boat, watching quietly as the sun dipped below the horizon. Ole finally asked, "Now what do we do?"

Sven shook his head. "I just wish we would have brought some paint."

"What are ya talking about?" asked Ole.

"Well, Ole, don't ya see? We could paint an "X" on da bottom of da boat, so we can find dis spot next time. We're commin back with more a dat cheese bait."

Ole laughs. "Sven, don't be such a dummy! Next time, what if dey give us a different boat?"

Hopefully, if you're doing any monster hunting soon, you don't fall into the troubles that our poor friends Sven and Ole ran into. Or at least make sure you don't go hunting with anyone named Sven or Ole.

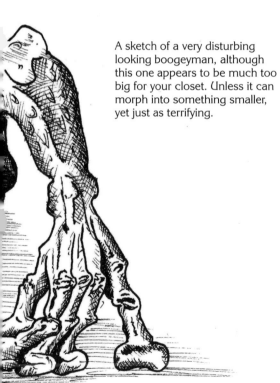

A sketch of a very disturbing looking boogeyman, although this one appears to be much too big for your closet. Unless it can morph into something smaller, yet just as terrifying.

But it brings up a good point. Regardless of how crazy all of this may sound, isn't it worth it to try and find out more? Maybe, just maybe, monsters are real. Wouldn't you like to be the one to find out? And perhaps you could start with some simple monsters, such as the Hodag from our cheese-head neighbors to the east of us, in Rhinelander, Wisconsin.

The Hodag, only found in the Rhinelander area of Wisconsin, was originally reported in the newspapers back in 1893. It has "the head of a frog, the grinning face of a giant elephant, thick short legs set off by huge claws, the back of a dinosaur, and a long tail with spears at the end." I've been to Rhinelander a few times, and have seen the Hodag, er, statues of it at least. So it must be real, right?

Like it or not, there's at least evidence of people who believe in monsters. The physical proof may not be there, but the word of mouth, the person with the story, is. And I often wonder, why would someone make this stuff up? Why lie about monsters? The world is sometimes scary enough, why add to it? No, I think in most cases, people see something, but it may be only in their mind.

Yet monsters of the mind can be just as scary. All it takes is a brief thought about Jason from *Friday the 13th*, or the evil character from the *Saw* movies. That can send chills down your spine, and make you think, if only for a moment, that these monsters are real.

And is there any possibility, that the things within our mind, actually create the creatures, bringing them into the real world? One would think not. But some physicists have indicated there is the potential for our thoughts to trigger events in the real world, at least at a quantum physics level. The power of intention may in fact be real, with the thoughts in our heads transcending into reality. If this is the case, we must be more careful at what we think. Especially if we continue with our researching of monsters like werewolves, vampires, witches, and warlocks. What once was fabricated fables, could now become terrorizing truths.

It seems as though the scientific community is only beginning to research the relationship between the mind and body, not to mention spirit. Many people when asked if they believe in spirit, and are religious, they answer yes. So, if that's the case, then it wouldn't be hard to recognize one could believe that your thoughts might turn into something physical. Although I would think this is very difficult to prove. It's probably up there with trying to track a Bigfoot that is a multi-dimensional being, shifting in and out of our world at will.

Regardless of your beliefs, wouldn't it behoove you to at least contemplate whether or not monsters exist? And maybe check out a few things in your neck of the woods. The next time your local newspaper reports on Bigfoot, a Wendigo, or maybe the Mothman, why not spend a few minutes and check into it? You may be surprised at what you find.

I'm sitting here, sipping on a Monster energy drink, both happy and sad that this book's journey is nearly over. "Zombie Zoo" by Tom Petty is playing in the background, shuffled randomly from my iTunes library. Pretty ironic if you

A werewolf drawing, quite possibly
similar to ones running around
southeastern Minnesota and
central Wisconsin.

ask me. But then things don't always happen by chance, do they?
There's usually a reason to everything. Like the reason you picked
up this book. Do you have any monsters in your closet? Do you have
questions about the unknown?

I know I do. And hopefully this book has helped you become
more aware about the mysterious, shadowy, lurking things of the
night. Perhaps it has changed you in some way, allowing you to
step across the frightful threshold between reality and the unknown,
bringing you a little closer to the impossible and improbable, making
you feel a tad bit more comfortable with it. And in many cases, that's
why we have books, why we exchange information. We are all trying
to become a little more than what we once were, trying to grow our
awareness into a blossoming blissful splendor of truth and comfort.
Although sometimes we're just trying to get away from it all, to escape
from the knowledge we've acquired and dive blindly into the abyss

of unfamiliarity, unidentifiable madness, with our only fear stemming from a life not lived. Which position are you in—why are you reading this book?

And are you a believer of frightful, fiendish monsters now? I mean, after all the stories, histories, and field trips, your mind must have changed somehow, right? If anything, I'm hoping you're now open to a greater awareness, expanding into something more. The unknown might be a little more known to you, which to me, is part of growing and becoming more than what you once were.

Warren Zevon's "Werewolves Of London" is playing now. A perfect song to end the book with. That, and with a few light-hearted monster jokes:

Q: Why did the monster eat a light bulb?
A: Because he was in need of a light snack.

Q: Do monsters eat popcorn with their fingers?
A: NO, they eat the fingers separately.

Q: What is the best way to speak to a monster?
A: From a long way away.

Q: What is a lake monster's favorite dish?
A: Fish and ships.

Q: What do you say to a two-headed monster?
A: Hello hello.

Q: Did you hear about the monster who had eight arms?
A: He said they came in handy.

As for me, I now have a greater appreciation for the unknown. When I go on my nightly dog walks, with my two golden retrievers, Sophi and Stanley, I keep an eye out for the things moving in the darkness. I didn't do much of that before writing this book. Now, well, I look to see if a giant cougar is pounding its way up the street behind me. Or if a demonic hellhound/werewolf, running with the local coyotes, gallops at me with evil intent from the neighbor's yard. And let's not forget about the Mothman, who may be hovering high above me, waiting for the right moment to pounce.

But please, do not be afraid of the unknown – it is your friend. The things in which we do not know about, often tend to keep us alive. They are the sparks of life that ignite our spirit, thrilling us and making us want more. And perhaps our next manifest destiny is a journey into the supernatural world. Will you go? It could be fun. Then again, it could be the last thing you ever do.

Regardless of how much we delve into that which is unknown, it will always be there, in my opinion. I very much doubt we will ever solve all the mysteries, and perhaps Bigfoot will always elude us, or a new Bigfoot will arise, daring us into the darkness beyond. Still, we must move forward; some of us must carry the beastly baton into the monstrous battle for truth and knowledge. Will that be you? Are you willing to brave the dark forests of northern Minnesota, camping in the middle of nowhere, and tromping through the trees, night-vision camera steadily in hand?

Let's not forget, too, that the monsters are not just in the rural sections of the state, running quietly through the sparsely populated prairies and woods, but also inhabit the cities of concrete, glass, and steel. The cougars of Bloomington, shadow people of Richfield—to name a few, apparently live among us in our continuous urban sprawl.

So the next time you take the garbage out late at night, look twice before you exit the safety of your home. You may be stepping into the world of the unknown, one that may soon become a little too normal for you (and not by your own doing). You will then shuffle and dance along a fine thread between life and death, comfort and fear, the known and unknown. Are you willing to take that chance? Or should you remain boxed up in that comfy chair you watch the world from. The choice is yours (most of the time). Choose wisely.

SOURCES

American Bear Association, www.americanbear.org

Arment, Chad. "Black panthers in North America." North American Bio-Fortean Review 3 (2000).

Arment, Chad. Cryptozoology: Science & Speculation. Coachwhip Publications, 2004.

Bear Attacks, www.bearplanet.org.

Bigfoot Field Researchers Organization, www.bfro.net.

California Academy of Sciences, www.research.calacademy.org/ichthyology.

Clark, Jerome, and Loren Coleman. Creatures of the Outer Edge. New York: Warner Books, 1978.

Coleman, Loren, and Patrick Huyghe. Field Guide to Lake Monsters, Sea Serpents, and Other Mystery Denizens of the Deep. New York: Tarcher/Penguin, 2003.

Coleman, Loren. Bigfoot! New York: Paraview Pocket Books, 2003.

Coleman, Loren and Jerome Clark. Cryptozoology A To Z: New York: Fireside, 1999.

"Cougar Spotted In Champlin Causes Quite The Stir." Gilbertson WCCO (December 2009).

"Deformed Frogs in Minnesota." Minnesota Pollution Control Agency, www.pca.state.mn.us.

"Fish Bites Boy." Cook Duluth News Tribune (2004).

Francis, Scott. Monster Spotter's Guide to North America. How, 2007.

Heinan, Joseph. Minnesota Bigfoot. www.angelfire.com/mn2/mnbf/. 1999-2007.

"Hoop Snake." www.en.wikipedia.org.

"I Believe in You." Burger www.kevynbaby.blogspot.com

My Fishing Pals Forum, www.myfishingpals.com

"Musky Attack." Rinzel, www.weau.com (2007).

"New Minnesota Mothman Sighting." Coleman www.cryptomundo.com (2007).

Paul Bunyan American Folklore, www.americanfolkloare.net.

Paul Bunyan and Babe the Blue Ox, www.en.wikipedia.org.

Smithsonian Institution North American Mammals, www.mnh.si.edu/mna.

Storm, Rory. Monster Hunt: The Guide to Cryptozoology. Sterling, 2008.

"The Creature from Lake Pepin." Harter, www.TwinCities.com (2008).

"The Legend of Pepie." Nielson, www.pepie.net.

"The Unexplained: The Vampire Myth." A&E DVD (2001).

"The Wendigo." Taylor, www.prairieghosts.com.

"Wendigo." www.en.wikipedia.org.

Wendigo." www.nativeonline.com.

"Why Not Cougars?" Breining, www.dnr.state.mn.us.

"Wizards in the Woods?" Korczak, www.unexplained-mysteries.com (2007).